Listening / Speaking	Reading / Writing	*KnowHow*
➤ **Listening:** People at a wedding ➤ **Speaking:** Talking about the people in your life	➤ **Reading:** *Real Talk* - an online conversation ➤ **Writing:** Having an "online" conversation	➤ Sentence stress
➤ **Listening:** How do they get to work? ➤ **Speaking:** Discussing a transportation questionnaire	➤ **Reading:** • *How the World Moves* • *Ride a bike in Helsinki* ➤ **Writing:** Describing a trip	➤ Pronunciation of *-s* endings
➤ **Listening:** Radio announcements ➤ **Speaking:** Discussing different kinds of music	➤ **Reading:** *Music is good for you!* ➤ **Writing:** Writing and responding to invitations	➤ Making vocabulary notes
➤ **Listening:** Renting a vacation home ➤ **Speaking:** Describing and renting a vacation home	➤ **Reading:** • *An Unusual Office* • *Unhappy? Try changing the furniture.* ➤ **Writing:** Describing a house	➤ Working in pairs
➤ **Listening:** Airport conversations ➤ **Speaking:** Describing people in a picture	➤ **Reading:** *The World's Largest Mall* ➤ **Writing:** Describing activities	➤ Pronunciation of *-ing* endings
➤ **Listening:** Time management ➤ **Speaking:** • Discussing the "good old days" • Taking a survey about being on time	➤ **Writing:** Describing a typical morning ➤ **Reading:** *It's about time!*	➤ Pronunciation of *-ed* endings
➤ **Listening:** Traditional diets ➤ **Speaking:** • Discussing diet and health • Creating a menu and ordering in a restaurant	➤ **Reading:** • *Shop Smart in the Supermarket* • *No More Couch Potatoes!* ➤ **Writing:** Describing eating habits	➤ Dictionary tips
➤ **Speaking:** Telling a story ➤ **Listening:** Song – "Silhouettes"	➤ **Reading:** *Squirrel helps police find stolen goods* ➤ **Writing:** Telling a story	➤ Vocabulary through reading

Contents

Listening / Speaking	Reading / Writing	KnowHow
➤ **Listening:** Life in Chicago, U.S. and Santiago, Chile ➤ **Speaking:** Discussing opinions	➤ **Reading:** *Survey Finds The Happiest Place* ➤ **Writing:** Preparing a travel brochure	➤ Word stress
➤ **Listening:** A guide dog trainer ➤ **Speaking:** Choosing an ideal job	➤ **Reading:** • *A Head for Heights* • *Telecommuting* ➤ **Writing:** A message to an online forum on telecommuting	➤ Listening tips
➤ **Listening:** An attorney talks about clothes ➤ **Speaking:** Making suggestions about clothes	➤ **Writing:** Describing a person ➤ **Reading:** *The Rose*	➤ Intonation in questions
➤ **Speaking:** • Choosing summer classes • Discussing priorities ➤ **Listening:** Burned out at 25	➤ **Reading:** *Students for life* ➤ **Writing:** Describing future plans	➤ Writing tips
➤ **Listening:** Who introduced Carol to Patrick? ➤ **Speaking:** Describing a good friend	➤ **Reading:** *Singles Find a New Place to Meet* ➤ **Writing:** Describing a person you know	➤ Speaking tips
➤ **Speaking:** • Discussing the impact of technology • Making predictions ➤ **Listening:** How do people use computers?	➤ **Writing:** Predicting changes in the future ➤ **Reading:** *Intelligent Clothing*	➤ Pronunciation of contractions with *will*
➤ **Listening:** Song – "In My Life" ➤ **Speaking:** Talking about interesting past experiences	➤ **Reading:** *No Fear of Flying* ➤ **Writing:** Greeting card messages	➤ Irregular verb forms
➤ **Speaking:** Taking a survey about free time activities ➤ **Listening:** Parts of the body and instructions	➤ **Writing:** Comparing interests and hobbies ➤ **Reading:** *A Vehicle for Their Art*	➤ Pronunciation of /s/ and /ʃ/

1 Meeting and greeting

✔ Social expressions and relationships
✔ Possessives; subject pronouns and *be*

1 ▶ Language in Action: Social expressions

a Introduce yourself.

    Example   *Hi. My name is Elisa.*

b `AUDIO` Listen. Then read.

  1 What is the woman's first name? _____

  2 What is her last name? _____

Good morning. It's seven o'clock. And this is...

Sally: Good morning, Ben.
Ben: Morning, Ms. Black. Allow me...
Sally: Thank you.
Ben: You're welcome.

Scott: Hi, Sally. How are you?
Sally: I'm fine, thanks.

Jack: My name is Jack Davis and this is Rosa Vargas. We're from the ONET office.
Sally: Hi, I'm Sally Black. Nice to meet you.

Sally: Goodbye, Scott. See you tomorrow.
Scott: Good night, Sally.

▼ Help Desk

Forms of address:

Men:

Mr. Davis

Women:

Mrs. Vargas (married)

Miss Johnston (single)

Ms. Black (married or single)

c Match an expression (1–5) with a response (a–e).

1	Good morning.	<u>1b</u>	a Hi. Nice to meet you.
2	How are you?	__	b Good morning.
3	Thank you.	__	c Goodbye.
4	My name is Jack Davis.	__	d I'm fine, thanks. And you?
5	See you tomorrow.	__	e You're welcome.

2 ⟩ KnowHow: Sentence stress

a AUDIO Listen to the expressions below. The dot indicates the main stress.

Good mȯrning.   How are you?   I'm fiṅe, thanks.   And yoū?

b AUDIO Now listen to the expressions. Mark the stressed word or syllable in each one.

Thaṅk you.	You're welcome.	My name is Jack.
Nice to meet you.	Goodbye.	See you tomorrow.

c Work with a partner. A, say a phrase from 1c. B, give a response.

3 ⟩ Focus on Grammar

a Look at the chart. Which word is the same in the singular and plural?

Possessives

Possessive adjectives

My name is Sally Black.	**Our** names are Sally and Scott.
Her name is Rosa Vargas.	
His name is Jack Davis.	**Their** names are Rosa and Jack.
Its name is ONET.	
What's **your** name?	What are **your** names?

Possessive 's

Rosa's last name is Vargas.	**Jack's** last name is Davis.

---

b Look at the photograph and complete the paragraph with words from the list.

his (2x)   our   her (2x)
my   their   mother's

Michael Price   Barbara Cooper   Cooper Price

¹ *My* friend Barbara and ² _____ family have non-traditional names. Barbara's last name is Cooper. Michael is ³ _____ husband, and ⁴ _____ last name is Price. ⁵ _____ son is three years old. ⁶ _____ first name is Cooper. So, his first name is his ⁷ _____ last name. Barbara says, "For some people, ⁸ _____ names are confusing. But we think they are interesting."

c Work with a partner. Introduce yourselves. Then talk about your classmates.

Example   A: *What's his name?* —B: *Alberto.*
          A: *What's Alberto's last name?* —B: *I don't know.*

4 ▶ In Conversation

AUDIO Where are Tom and Anita from? Listen. Then read.

Matt: Donna! Hi!
Donna: Matt! What a surprise! How are you?
Matt: I'm fine. And you?
Donna: Great. It's good to see you! Oh, I'm sorry. This
is Tom Osumi and this is his wife Anita. Tom,
I'd like you to meet my cousin Matt.
Matt: It's nice to meet you. Where are you from?
Tom: We're from Vancouver.

5 ▶ Focus on Grammar

a What are the full forms of the underlined words? Look at the chart and check your
answers.

<u>I'm</u> fine. <u>We're</u> from Vancouver. <u>It's</u> nice to meet you.

Subject pronouns and *be*		
Affirmative		**Negative**
I'm (I am) **You're** (You are) **He's / She's / It's** (He is…) **We're / They're** (We are…)	from Canada.	**I'm not** (I am not) **You aren't** (You are not) **He / She / It isn't** (He is not…) **We / They aren't** (We are not…)
Questions		**Answers**
Are you from Mexico? Where **are you** from? **Is Tom** from Japan? Where **is he** from? **Are Tom and Anita** from England? Where **are they** from?		No, **I'm not**. / Yes, **I am**. Hong Kong. No, **he isn't**. / Yes, **he is**. Canada. No, **they're not**. / Yes, **they are**. Canada.

In the negative section, "from Japan." appears to the right of the rows.

b Complete the conversation with the correct form of *be*. Use contractions where possible.

Scott: Hi. Would you like something to drink?
Cindy: Oh, yes, thank you.
Scott: You're __¹ welcome. Oh—I ____² sorry.
My name ____³ Scott Atkinson.
Cindy: I ____⁴ Cindy Mendez. This ____⁵ my husband, Larry.
Scott: Nice to meet you. Where ____⁶ you from?
Cindy: We ____⁷ from California.
Scott: Really? What part?
Cindy: Sonoma.
Scott: ____⁸ that near Los Angeles?
Cindy: No, it ____⁹. It ____¹⁰ near San Francisco.

▼ **Help Desk**

Note that *you* is singular
and plural.

*Are **you** from Japan?*

*Yes, **I** am.* Or *Yes, **we** are.*

c Work in groups of three. Practice the conversation. Use different names and places.

6 Reading

a Brian and Kira are chatting online. Put their conversation in order. Write the numbers 1–9 in the blanks.

Location http://www.RealTalk.khw

Mail   Calendar   Download

Real Talk

___ Brian:
I'm from Australia,
but I'm in Washington right now.

_1_ Brian:
Hi everybody.

___ Kira:
Oh, OK. Do you live there?

___ Brian:
No, Washington State.
It's in the northwest.

___ Kira:
I'm from Peru. What about you?

___ Brian:
Nice to meet you, too!
Where are you from, Kira?

___ Kira:
Washington, D.C.?
The capital of the United States?

___ Kira
Hi Brian.
Nice to meet you!

___ Brian:
No. I'm on vacation. My sister
is a student at Seattle University.

b Make six true sentences. Use the words in the box and *be* or *be* + *not*.

Example   *Brian is from Australia.*

Brian Brian's sister Brian and his sister Kira	from Australia from Peru in Washington, D.C. in Washington State at Seattle University

7 Writing

Work with a partner on the other side of the room. A, write a note to your partner, and pass it across the room. B, answer your partner's note on the same piece of paper. Create a conversation like the one in 6a.

Here are some questions that you can ask:

Where are you from?   **Where is that?**
Are you a student?   **What about you?**

Hi! My name is Tony.

Hi Tony. Where are you from?

8 Vocabulary: People in your life

a Look at the photographs. Write the letter of the correct picture next to each expression.

1 brothers and sisters _D_   3 neighbors __   5 boyfriend and girlfriend __
2 friends __   4 colleagues __   6 parents __

b Make sentences about the people in the pictures above.

Example *He's a neighbor. They're parents.*

c Match words 1–8 with words a–h. Which word does not change?

MEN		WOMEN
1 father	_1e_	a aunt
2 son	__	b cousin
3 brother-in-law	__	c daughter
4 cousin	__	d grandmother
5 uncle	__	e mother
6 nephew	__	f sister-in-law
7 husband	__	g wife
8 grandfather	__	h niece

▼ **Help Desk**

Irregular plurals

person	people
man	men
woman	women
child	children

d Work with a partner. **A**, describe one of the people in the diagram. **B**, guess the person.

Example A: *He's Adam's father.*
        B: *Michael.*

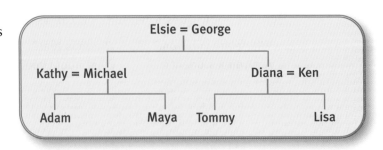

5

9 Listening

a Look at the picture of a wedding. Look at the names below.
Who do you think the people are?

Joe   Emily   Alan   Alan's wife   Alan's daughter

Betty

b [AUDIO] Listen. Which person on the list in 9a is **not** in the picture?

c [AUDIO] Listen again. Write T (true) or F (false).

1 Betty is Joe's sister.   *F*
2 Alan is Joe's colleague.   __
3 Alan isn't from California.   __
4 Alan's wife is American.   __
5 Alan's wife is at the party.   __

d Who do people usually invite to weddings?

10 Speaking

a Work with a partner. On a piece of paper, write the names of five people in your life (family, friends, colleagues). Give the paper to your partner.

b Take turns. Ask and answer questions about the people. Say as much as you can.

Example
A: *Who's Tom Vega?*
B: *He's my neighbor. He's from Costa Rica. His wife's name is Sandy. She's American.*

2 From here to there

✔ Transportation and travel
✔ Simple present

1 ▷ Reading

a Read the paragraphs. How do these people go to work? Fill in the blanks.

1 Ben ___*train*___ _____
2 Pierre and Arlette _____
3 Ming _____

How the World Moves

Ben Wilson takes a train from his home in Manhattan. On the train, he usually makes telephone calls or works on his computer. Then he takes a taxi from the train station to his office. He doesn't have time to walk.

Pierre and Arlette Gigot get up at five-thirty, and take two buses to their jobs in Paris. They don't talk much on the bus. Arlette often sleeps, and Pierre reads the newspaper.

Ming Li takes a ferry across Victoria Harbor every morning to her job in Hong Kong. It takes about ten minutes, and Ming enjoys the boat ride. She listens to music, relaxes, and looks at the view. "It's a wonderful way to get to work," she says.

b Write the correct name(s) in each blank.

Ben   Pierre and Arlette   Ming

1 _____ works in Hong Kong.
2 _____ lives in Manhattan.
3 _____ get up very early.
4 _____ takes a train and a taxi.
5 _____ take two buses.
6 _____ likes the ride to work.

2 ▷ Vocabulary: Transportation

a Look at the words below. Which kinds of transportation do you see in the pictures on this page?

| bicycle | bus | car | airplane | motorcycle |
| taxi | train | subway | cable car | ferry |

b Which kinds of transportation are popular where you live? Which are unusual?

3 Focus on Grammar

a Look at the sentences in 1b. Which verb forms end in -s? Which do not? Why?

Simple present: Statements

Affirmative		Negative	
I / You / We / They	**take** the bus.	I / You / We / They	**don't take** the ferry.
He / She	**takes** the ferry.	He / She	**doesn't take** the bus.
It	**takes** ten minutes.	It	**doesn't take** an hour.

Spelling: -s endings
- Add *-s* after most verbs: *lives, works*
- Add *-es* after *s, sh, ch, x, o*: *guesses, finishes, watches, relaxes, goes*
- Change *have* to *has*.   Change *y* to *i* and add *-es* after a consonant: *studies*

---

b Look at the chart. Circle the correct word in the sentences below.

1 My friend Paul (work / (works)) in Boston.
2 He (go / goes) to work on the train.
3 He (don't / doesn't) take the bus.
4 My husband and I (drive / drives) to work.
5 It doesn't (take / takes) a long time.
6 We (listen / listens) to music in the car.

c Complete the paragraph with the correct form of the verbs below.

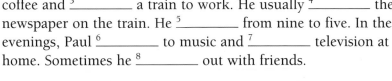

get up   take   read   listen   work   go   have   watch

Paul ¹ *gets up* at seven every morning. He ²_____ a cup of coffee and ³_____ a train to work. He usually ⁴_____ the newspaper on the train. He ⁵_____ from nine to five. In the evenings, Paul ⁶_____ to music and ⁷_____ television at home. Sometimes he ⁸_____ out with friends.

d How is your day different from Paul's? How is it the same?

Example   *I don't get up at 7:00. I get up at 7:30.*

4 KnowHow: Pronunciation of -s endings

a **AUDIO** Listen. Repeat the sentences. Practice the pronunciation of the final -s.

1 / z /   *lives*   Paul lives in Boston.   *listens*   He listens to music.
2 / s /   *takes*   Ben takes a train.   *gets*   He gets to work at eight.
3 / ɪz / *finishes*   Ben finishes at five.   *watches*   Paul watches television.

b Work with a partner. Talk about Claudia. Change *I* to *she*.

```
I teach English. I work at a high
school. I drive to work. I listen to
music in the car. I get to work at
eight. I finish work at three. I go
home and relax.
```

Example   *Claudia teaches English. She works…*

5 ▶ Vocabulary: Feelings

a Look at the picture. Make sentences about the people.

Example *He's hungry. She's bored.*

b Work with a partner. Ask and answer questions about the words above.

Example A: *When are you tired?*
B: *I'm tired after work.*

6 ▶ Listening

a AUDIO Listen to these people talking about their commute. How does each person get to work?

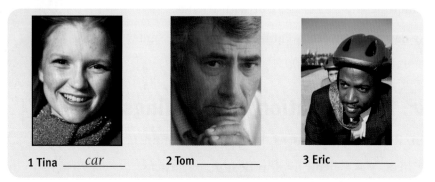

1 Tina ___*car*___   2 Tom _____   3 Eric _____

b AUDIO Listen again. Check the correct answer.

	Tina	Tom	Eric	
1	✓			drives a lot.
2				doesn't like the subway.
3				sometimes takes a bus.
4				doesn't have a car.
5				is tired after work.
6				listens to music.

c Which person are you like: Tina, Tom, or Eric?

Focus on Grammar

a Look at the chart. Fill in the blanks below.

1 The first word in a *yes/no* question is _____ or _____.
2 Negative short answers use the contractions _____ or _____.

Simple present: Questions					
Yes / No *questions*			**Short answers**		
Do	you	**take** the bus?		I	**do.**
Does	he	**drive** to work?	Yes, he	**does.**	No, he	**doesn't.**
Does	it	**take** an hour?	it	**does.**	it	**doesn't.**
Wh- *(information) questions*					
How	**do**	you	get to work?		
What	**does**	Ben	do on the train?		
How long	**does**	it	take?		

b **AUDIO** Put the words in order to make questions. Then listen and check your answers.

1 to / work / do / drive / you   *Do you drive to work?*
2 do / how / get / to / you / work   _____
3 does / how / it / long / take   _____
4 way / do / do / on / the / what / you   _____
5 your / have / a / does / city / subway   _____

c Work with a partner. Ask and answer the questions above.

Speaking

a Read and complete the questionnaire.

> **Transportation Questionnaire**
> *Please answer these questions. Thank you.*
>
> 1. What kinds of transportation do you use?
>   (Check all appropriate responses.)
>   ☐ car   ☐ motorcycle   ☐ bus   ☐ train
>   ☐ bicycle   ☐ walking   ☐ other: _____
> 2. Do you use public transportation?
>   ☐ Yes ☐ No
>   If yes, what kind of public transportation do you use?
>   ☐ bus ☐ train ☐ ferry ☐ subway ☐ other: _____
> 3. How long does the trip to work or school take?
>   ☐ 0-15 min. ☐ 15-30 min. ☐ 30-45 min. ☐ 45+ min.
> 4. What are some of the problems with public
>   transportation where you live? _____
>   _____
>
> *Thank you for your time.*

▼ **Help Desk**

Don't use *a* or *the* in these expressions:

go to work, go to school
(Not: *go to the work*)

Don't use *a, the,* or *to* in these expressions:

go home, go downtown
(Not: *go to home*)

b Work in small groups. Ask and answer the questions from the questionnaire. Make notes of the answers. What is the most popular form of transportation?

9 Reading

a Look at the pictures in the article. Why do people in cities ride bicycles?

b Read the article and choose the best summary.

1 People in Helsinki are often late for work.
2 Helsinki has a free bicycle program.
3 Helsinki is a good place to ride bicycles.

Ride a bike in Helsinki

You're late for work, and you don't have a car. The bus is too slow. What do you do? If you live in Helsinki, Finland, you can take a green bicycle from the street and ride it to work.

Helsinki's City Bike Program operates 26 bike stands in the center of Helsinki. Anyone can use them. You take a city bike from a stand and leave a small deposit. After you finish with the bicycle, you return it to a stand and get your money back.

The bicycles are simple but comfortable. They have a special design, and they are painted bright green, so it is easy to see them.

The program is very popular. For many people, a City Bike is a practical way to get around. All kinds of people use the bicycles: shoppers, elderly people, and students going to class.

There are free bike programs in several other cities also, including Copenhagen, Toronto, and Orlando.

c Read the article again. Write T (true) or F (false).

1 The City Bike stands are outside the city. ___
2 It costs a lot of money to use a City Bike. ___
3 All City Bikes are the same color. ___
4 Many people use the bicycles. ___
5 Some other cities have programs like this. ___

d Find a word in the article to complete each sentence. (1) = paragraph number.

1 You're not early. You're _____.(1)
2 The bus isn't fast. It's _____.(1)
3 The bicycles are nice to sit on. They're _____.(3)
4 Many people like the program. It's _____.(4)
5 You don't pay for the bikes. They're _____. (5)

e What do you think? Is this program a good idea?

10 ▶ Writing

a Read the paragraph. Where does Alicia go every summer? Why does she enjoy it?

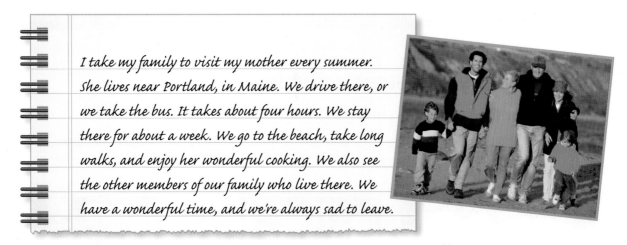

> *I take my family to visit my mother every summer. She lives near Portland, in Maine. We drive there, or we take the bus. It takes about four hours. We stay there for about a week. We go to the beach, take long walks, and enjoy her wonderful cooking. We also see the other members of our family who live there. We have a wonderful time, and we're always sad to leave.*

b Work with a partner. Ask and answer questions about a trip that you take regularly. Make notes of your partner's answers.

c Write a paragraph about your partner's trip. Then exchange papers. Is the information about you correct?

11 ▶ Language in Action: Travel talk

a **AUDIO** Complete the conversation using questions from the box. Then listen and check your answers.

Alicia: Excuse me.
Agent: Yes, can I help you?
Alicia: [1] *Is this the bus to Portland*_____?
Agent: Yes, it is.
Alicia: [2] _____?
Agent: 10:30.
Alicia: OK, thank you. Oh… [3] _____?
Agent: Four hours and ten minutes.
Alicia: Thank you very much.

> **ASKING FOR TRAVEL INFORMATION**
> • Is this the bus / train / flight / way to…?
> • When does it leave?
> • How long does it take?
> • How much does it cost?
> • How far is it?

b Work with a partner. Make conversations for the following situations. Use the questions in the box above and the information below each picture.

Amsterdam 11:45
two hours

O'Connell Street three euros
about twenty minutes

Middlefield
about twenty miles

12

3 On the go

✔ Activities and entertainment
✔ Adverbs of frequency, time, and place

1 Vocabulary: Free-time activities

a Write the letter of the correct picture next to each expression.

1 go to the movies _B_
2 stay home __
3 get together with friends __
4 listen to live music __
5 go to the gym __
6 go out dancing __

b Which activities do you like to do?

2 In Conversation

AUDIO How are Vera and Mike different? Listen. Then read.

Mike: So what do you do for entertainment?
Vera: Oh, not much. I get together with friends and talk.
Mike: How often do you do that?
Vera: Oh, about four times a week.
Mike: That's a lot.
Vera: That's just during the week. On weekends I usually go out dancing. We sometimes stay out until 4:00 a.m.
Mike: Wow! I hardly ever stay out that late. And I'm always busy during the week.
Vera: Why is that?
Mike: Oh, I have a class twice a week, and I often go to the gym after work.

▼ **Help Desk**

The expression *go out* sometimes refers to social activities.

*How often do you **go out**?*

*I like to **go out** dancing.*

*We **go out** to eat.*

13

3 ▶ Focus on Grammar

a Look at the words. Put them in order of frequency.

always   hardly ever   never   often   sometimes   usually

least frequent ──────────────────────────────▶ most frequent
1 _never_   2 _____   3 _sometimes_   4 _____   5 _____   6 _____

b Look at the chart below and circle the correct answers below.

Adverbs of frequency usually come…
1 (before / after) *be*.
2 (before / after) other verbs.

Adverbs of frequency			**Other expressions of frequency**		
always	often	usually	once a week	twice a month	on weekends
sometimes	hardly ever	never	three times a year	during the week	
I **usually** stay out late. I am **always** busy.			I go to the movies **twice a month.** **Twice a month**, I go to the movies.		

Note: In negative sentences, adverbs usually go between the auxiliary and the main verb:
*I don't **usually** stay out late.*

c Rewrite these sentences with the expressions in parentheses. Then check your answers with a partner.

1 On weekends, I go out dancing. (usually)   _On weekends, I usually go out dancing._
2 We stay out late. (sometimes)   _____
3 I stay out so late. (hardly ever)   _____
4 I don't go out during the week. (usually)   _____
5 I'm busy! (always)   _____
6 I have a class. (twice a week)   _____

d Work with a partner. Ask questions about how often you do these things.

Example   A: *How often do you get together with friends?*
          B: *About twice a week. What about you?*

get together with friends   go to the movies
go to English class   go shopping for clothes
go out to eat   use a computer

> ▼ **Help Desk**
>
> *A lot* and *not (very) much* are informal expressions of frequency.
>
> *We go out **a lot**.* (= often)
>
> *We **don't** go to restaurants **very much**.* (= not often)

4 Vocabulary: Entertainment

a Look at the pictures. List the types of entertainment in the categories below.

Usually outdoors	Usually indoors	Have live music	Good for children
Festivals			

b Work with a partner. Compare your answers. Do you agree?

c Which types of entertainment do you enjoy? Why?

a festival

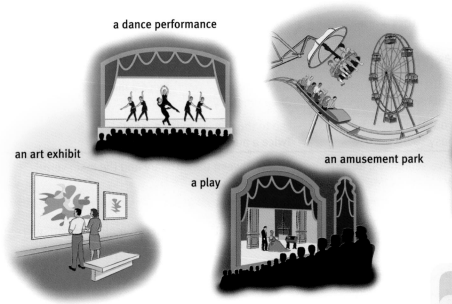

a dance performance

an art exhibit

a play

an amusement park

a rock concert

▼ **Help Desk**

Play can be a noun or a verb.

You watch **a play** in the theater, but you **play** baseball or tennis.

5 Listening

a What kinds of entertainment are in the advertisements (ads)?

b AUDIO Listen. Number the events below in the order you hear them.

c AUDIO Listen again. You will hear four mistakes in the radio announcement. Circle the correct information below.

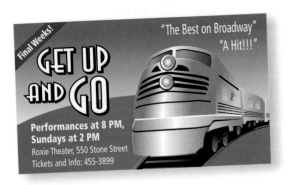

Final Weeks!

"The Best on Broadway"
"A Hit!!!"

GET UP AND GO

Performances at 8 PM,
Sundays at 2 PM
Roxie Theater, 550 Stone Street
Tickets and Info: 455-3899

Summer in the City Celebration

10 AM to 6 PM

July 14 and 15
Food · Live music · Magic shows

Franklin Park (Corner of Main and Broadway)

Della Thompson Sings the Blues

Saturday, July 14,
9 p.m.

Tickets: Delta Records
or Ticketrax: (702)555-7000
$15 ($12 students)

BLUE MOON CLUB, 420 Blake Street

6 ▸ Focus on Grammar

a Look at the chart. Which come first—expressions of time or expressions of place?

Adverbial phrases of time and place

Placement of adverbial phrases

The musical is **at the Roxie Theater at 8:oo p.m.**
It's **at Franklin Park on Saturday and Sunday.**
Della Thompson performs **at the Blue Moon Club at 9:00 p.m.**

Prepositions in adverbial phrases

• Use *at* with time. *at 8:oo p.m.*
• Use *on* with days and dates. *on Saturday, on the fourteenth*
• Use *in* with morning / afternoon / evening, but *at* with night.
  in the afternoon, at night

---

b Add an adverb of frequency, a time, and a place to each sentence. Write true sentences.

1 I watch TV.   *I usually watch TV at home in the evenings.*
2 I visit friends.   _____
3 I talk on the phone.   _____
4 I have an English class. _____
5 I go shopping.   _____
6 I listen to music.   _____

c Work with a partner. Compare your sentences. What do you have in common?

7 ▸ *KnowHow*: Making vocabulary notes

a Writing notes on new vocabulary will help you use it with confidence.
Look at the example from a student's notebook.

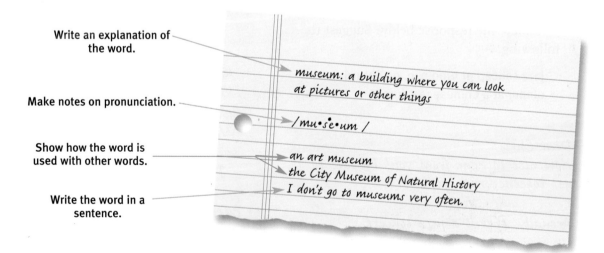

Write an explanation of the word.

Make notes on pronunciation.

Show how the word is used with other words.

Write the word in a sentence.

museum: a building where you can look at pictures or other things

/mu•se•um /

an art museum
the City Museum of Natural History
I don't go to museums very often.

b Make notes about these words.

   amusement park   performance   exhibit

Language in Action: Arrangements

a AUDIO What are Brandon and Grace going to do?
Listen. Then read.

Brandon: Let's get together this weekend.
Grace: That sounds good.
Brandon: There's a blues concert at the Plaza on
Saturday evening. Would you like to go?
Grace: Sounds great! I love the blues. Where
would you like to meet?
Brandon: Let's meet at Dante's. Then we can eat first.
Grace: That's a good idea. What time?
Brandon: Umm…how about 7:00?
Grace: OK. See you at Dante's at 7:00.

b Complete the phrases in the chart with examples from the conversation.

INVITING AND SUGGESTING	AGREEING	SAYING NO
Would you like to _____?	OK.	I'm sorry. I can't.
Let's _____.	That's a good idea.	Sorry. I'm busy.
How about _____?	(That) sounds great.	I'd like to, but…

c Make arrangements to do things with three different people this weekend. (Choose events
from page 15, or use your own ideas.) Arrange times and places to meet. If you can't go,
suggest a different event, time, or place.

Writing

a Read the note from Chris. What does he
want to do?

b Complete the response below. Suggest the
following:

**jazz concert at 9:00 p.m. on Saturday
dinner at a Chinese restaurant**

Dear Chris:
How nice to hear from you! I'd love to
get together with you.

Actually, there's a jazz concert

Hi!
How are you? I hope everything is
OK with you.
Guess what? We're going to be
in your area from Thursday, July
16th, to Sunday the 19th! We'd
love to see you, if possible. Would
you like to get together one evening?
We can go out to eat or listen to
some live jazz!
I hope you're free. Let me know.

Best wishes,
Chris

c Write a note inviting a classmate to an event.
Then read and respond to each other's notes.

10 ▶ Reading

a Look at the headline. What do you think? How is music good for you? Think of two ways.

b Read the article. Find four ways music helps people.

Music is good for you!

Do you need to get off the sofa and go to the gym? If you want to get motivated to exercise, try listening to your favorite songs or to dance music.

Psychologists at Brunel University in London say that certain types of music help people to get started and also to exercise for a longer time. People who listen to music exercise for 13 percent longer than people who don't. International athletes often listen to music when they are training.

Doctors know about the therapeutic effects of music. Listening to music can help people recover after operations. Teachers should pay attention, too. In a study at the University of California, students who took a test while listening to a Mozart sonata scored 30 percent higher than students who took the test in silence.

Music also relaxes people after a stressful day. Pauline Etkin, director of a music therapy center in London, says that throughout life's ups and downs, people always respond to music. When someone is nervous or afraid, it can make them feel better. "Music's rhythm is closely linked with the rhythms of the body," she says.

c Find a word in the article that means the following. (1) = paragraph number.

1 people who play sports (2): _____
2 to get better after being sick (3): _____
3 scared (4): _____
4 a regular pattern in sound or music (4): _____

11 ▶ Speaking

a Work in small groups. Add other kinds of music to the list.

classical music   jazz   rock   (others) _____

b Discuss the questions.

1 What kinds of music do you like? What kinds don't you like?
2 How often do you listen to music?
3 What kinds of music are good or not good in the following situations?

at the gym   at work   at home   at a party   at the supermarket   in the car

4 Personal spaces

✔ Homes and furniture
✔ *There is / are; this, that, these, those*

1 ▶ Reading

a Read the paragraph about Pete Nelson's office. Why does he like it?

b Read the paragraph again. Which of the following are in the tree house?

desks   a computer   a bed
a sofa   an armchair

c Work with a partner. Discuss the questions.

1 Would you like to live or work in a tree house?
2 Where do you spend the most time at home?

kitchen   office   living room
dining room   bedroom

An Unusual Office

My office is in a tree house outside my home in Seattle. It's a great place to work. There are a lot of windows, so it's very bright. There are two desks, a computer, and a comfortable armchair for reading. There's also a bed for visitors. When my friends visit, they always ask to stay in the tree house. It's small, but it's quiet and relaxing, and it has a beautiful view.

2 ▶ Focus on Grammar

a Look at the chart. Underline expressions with *there* in the paragraph above.

There **is** / *are*	
Singular	**Plural**
There is a bed in the tree house.	**There are** a lot of windows.
There isn't a sofa.	**There aren't** a lot of beds.
Is there an armchair? Yes, **there is**. / No, **there isn't**.	**Are there** a lot of windows? Yes, **there are**. / No, **there aren't**.
Note: There is = There's	

▼ **Help Desk**

Don't confuse *there are* and *they are*.

There are three bedrooms in my apartment.

They (the bedrooms) *are* on the second floor.

b Rewrite the sentences. Use *There is / isn't* or *There are / aren't*.

1 My office has two desks.   *There are two desks in my office.*
2 A lot of books and papers are on my desk. _____
3 My office doesn't have a lot of pictures. _____
4 A large plant is in the corner. _____
5 It doesn't have a view. _____

c **AUDIO** Listen and check your answers.

3 ▶ Vocabulary: Furniture and prepositions of location (place)

a Work with a partner. Look at the picture. Fill in the blanks with the words.

door   wall   window   table   television   chair   sofa

1	_____
2	_____
3	_____
4	_____
5	stove
6	sink
7	refrigerator
8	_____
9	rug
10	coffee table
11	_____
12	lamp
13	_____
14	blinds
15	bookcase

b Read the sentences below. Fill in the blanks with words from the picture above.

1 There are _____ on the window in the living room.
2 The _____ is in one corner of the kitchen.
3 The _____ is between the stove and the refrigerator.
4 There's a _____ in front of the sofa in the living room.
5 There's a _____ next to the sofa.
6 There's a _____ next to the table in the living room.
7 There's a _____ under the table.

c Work with a partner. Describe the location of these items. Use prepositions.

Example   table / window
          The table is in front of the window.

1 lamp / table
2 rug / table
3 refrigerator / sink

4 pictures / wall
5 coffee table / sofa
6 television / sofa

d Work with a partner. Describe a room you know well.

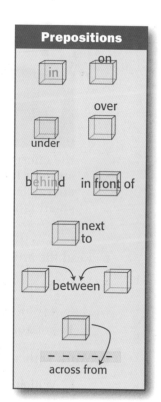

20

4 ▶ Reading

a Look at the pictures. Which items would you like to have in your living room?

a glass table   a sharp edge   a wooden table   a rounded corner   a metal file cabinet

b Read the article. Which of these is a *Feng Shui* principle?

   a   A lot of furniture makes a room clean and neat.

   b   The arrangement of a room affects health and happiness.

Unhappy? Try changing the furniture. HEALTH & HOME

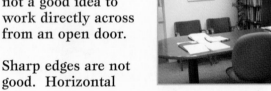

ARE YOU UNLUCKY IN LOVE or unhappy at work? Maybe you should change the arrangement of furniture in your home or office. According to the traditional Chinese philosophy of *Feng Shui*, changes in physical environment can affect our health and happiness. Here is some advice that can make a difference.

First, keep rooms clean and neat. Too much stuff, like furniture, books, clothes, or papers, blocks the energy. If your front door is in a straight line with the back door, the energy leaves the house too quickly. Put a small table or a plant near the door to slow it down. It's also not a good idea to work directly across from an open door.

Sharp edges are not good. Horizontal window blinds, for example, "cut up" the energy in a room. Don't sit across from a sharp corner. Use furniture with rounded corners and edges, especially in living rooms and bedrooms. Don't use a lot of metal or glass furniture.

Balance the different kinds of energy in a room. In a kitchen, where a sink is next to a stove, put something wooden between them. This balances the energies of fire and water. In an office, put a plant next to a computer to counteract the electromagnetic energy.

c Read the article again. Check the items that agree with *Feng Shui* principles.

   1 clean, organized spaces   ✓   4 rounded corners   —

   2 a desk across from an open door —   5 a sink next to a stove   —

   3 horizontal blinds   —   6 a plant near a computer   —

d Work with a partner. Look at the two offices in the photographs above. Discuss the questions.

   1 Which office illustrates good *Feng Shui*? Why?

   2 How would you change the other office according to *Feng Shui* principles?

   3 What do you think about the ideas in the article?

5 ⟩ In Conversation

AUDIO Where are Dan and Yvonne going to put the picture and the plants? Listen. Then read.

Dan: Where would you like to put this?

Yvonne: Put what?

Dan: This picture.

Yvonne: Oh, let's put it in a good place. How about over that bookcase?

Dan: No, it's too big.

Yvonne: Over the sofa?

Dan: OK. And what about those plants?

Yvonne: Let's put them over here next to the window. I can move these boxes.

Dan: OK.

6 ⟩ Focus on Grammar

a Check the correct boxes for each word in the chart below.

This, that, these, those

	Near	Far	Singular	Plural
this	✓		✓	
that				
these				
those		✓		

Where would you like to put	**this?** **this** plant?	What about	**these?** **these** plants?
Where would you like to put	**that?** **that** plant?	What about	**those?** **those** plants?

b Circle the correct word in the sentences below.

1 Come here and look at (these / those) flowers.
2 Who are (these / those) people over there?
3 Hello, Vera? (This / That) is Sandy. Please call me at 453-0788.
4 Sit here. (This / That) chair isn't very comfortable.
5 Hi. My name is Grace, and (these / those) are my friends, John and Sandra.
6 Let's watch a different movie. (This / That) one is terrible.
7 You live in New Haven? Where's (this / that)?
8 How much are (these / those) plants in that corner?

c Work with a partner. Ask and answer questions about objects and people in the room you're in. Use these questions:

What's this?   **What are these?**   **Who are those people?**   **Who's that?**

7 Writing

a In a home exchange program, people exchange homes in different places for a short time. Read the description of this home. Would you like to stay there?

Home Exchange International

HOME EXCHANGE INTERNATIONAL

▶ SCOTLAND

Our home is on a quiet road in the heart of Scotland. We are about 90 minutes from Edinburgh.

The house has six bedrooms, a dining room, a large living room, an office, a kitchen, and three bathrooms. There is a TV, a VCR, and a computer. There are beautiful views of the countryside from every room. We have a large garden with many beautiful plants. This is an excellent location for walking, golfing, and fishing.

NEXT ▶

b Work in pairs. Fill in the form about this house. Use your imagination! Then write a description of the house to advertise it on the Internet.

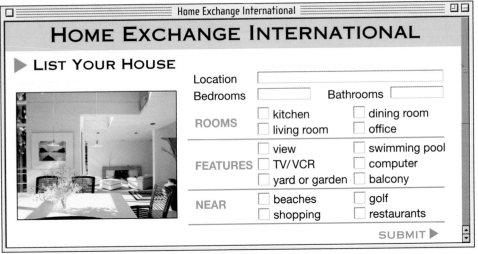

Home Exchange International

HOME EXCHANGE INTERNATIONAL

▶ LIST YOUR HOUSE

Location

Bedrooms   Bathrooms

ROOMS
☐ kitchen   ☐ dining room
☐ living room   ☐ office

FEATURES
☐ view   ☐ swimming pool
☐ TV/VCR   ☐ computer
☐ yard or garden   ☐ balcony

NEAR
☐ beaches   ☐ golf
☐ shopping   ☐ restaurants

SUBMIT ▶

c Exchange descriptions with another pair. Which description is the most attractive?

8 Listening

a [AUDIO] Listen. Ellen is calling for information about a house. Is she going to rent the house?

b [AUDIO] Listen again. What five things does Ellen ask about the house?

9 Language in Action: Clarification

a **AUDIO** Listen to part of the conversation in 8a. Check the expressions in the box that you hear in the conversation.

b Work with a partner. Ask and answer questions about one of the houses on page 23. Ask for clarification each time.

> Example A: *Where is the house?*
> B: *It's near Edinburgh.*
> A: *How do you spell that?*

Where is...?   **Does it have...?**
How many... are there?   **How far is it from...?**

> **ASKING FOR CLARIFICATION**
> __ Could you repeat that, please?
> __ Did you say... or...?
> __ How do you spell that?
> __ I'm sorry. I don't understand.

10 *KnowHow*: Working in pairs

Working in pairs or groups is an opportunity to practice speaking English. Here are some ideas for working with other students. Use these strategies in section 11.

1 Work with different partners.
2 Sit near enough to hear your partner.
3 If you don't understand your partner, ask for clarification!
4 Look at your partner when you speak, not at your notes or the book.

11 Speaking

a Work with a partner. Look at the photos of vacation rentals in Boston and Hawaii.

A, you would like to rent apartment 1 for one week. Look at the picture and make a list of questions to ask.
B, you are the owner of apartment 1. Complete the information about the apartment. Add extra information.

b A, call B and ask for information about the apartment. Begin like this:

B: *Hello.*
A: *Hi. I'm interested in the apartment for rent.*

c Reverse roles and do the task again with apartment 2.

HOME EXCHANGE INTERNATIONAL

Location: _____
Bedrooms: _____ Bathrooms: _____
Rooms:
☐ kitchen   ☐ dining room
☐ living room   ☐ office
Features:
☐ view   ☐ swimming pool
☐ TV/VCR   ☐ computer
☐ yard or garden   ☐ balcony
Near:
☐ beaches   ☐ golf
☐ shopping   ☐ restaurants

Grammar

1 Read the text. Where does Rafaela live? Where does she work?

BUSINESS PROFILE

Rafaela Orbieto is the president of a design company with offices in Caracas, Venezuela and Los Angeles, California. Because her business is in two places, Rafaela travels a lot and has homes in both cities. In Caracas she lives in a big apartment with her husband and their daughter. Twice a month she flies to Los Angeles. "Life in L.A. is very fast," she says. "I go out a lot for work, and I meet a lot of people. I also get to spend time with my son, who is a student there." What's the secret of her success? Rafaela says: "I love what I do. I'm never bored. There is always something exciting going on."

2 Complete the paragraph with subject pronouns or possessive adjectives.

¹ *My* name is Antonio Orbieto and ²____ 'm a student at UCLA in California. ³____ have one sister. ⁴____ name is Lisbeth, and ⁵____ lives in Caracas with ⁶____ parents. ⁷____ names are Rafaela and Eugenio, and ⁸____ are both busy professionals. ⁹____ family is very close, and ¹⁰____ get together often. I enjoy ¹¹____ life in California, but sometimes I miss ¹²____ home in Venezuela and ¹³____ pleasant atmosphere.

3 Complete the questions with *do / does* or *be* in the correct form. Then write true answers to the questions.

1 ___*Are*___ you from Brazil?
   No, I'm not. I'm from _____

2 _____ your friends go out a lot in the evening?
   _____

3 _____ your birthday in June?
   _____

4 How late _____ you usually sleep on the weekend?
   _____

5 _____ your friends enjoy art exhibits?
   _____

6 What time _____ you have English class?
   _____

4 Correct one mistake in each sentence.

1 Armand and Michelle are brother and sister. ~~They're~~ ^{Their} last name is Guyot.

2 Here is the calculator, and it's case is over there.

3 Susans mother is from Taipei, Taiwan.

4 There is papers on my desk.

5 Do you know Bob and Sally? Their my neighbors.

6 Mandy goes to home at 6 o'clock.

7 Please hand me those pencil. I can't reach it.

8 Paul isn't get together with his friends very often.

Vocabulary

5 Cross out the word in each group that is different.

1 neighbor sister nephew parent
2 concert window exhibit movie
3 taxi subway ferry school
4 bicycle table chair desk
5 ride like drive walk
6 thirsty long tired interested
7 next to between late under

Add at least one more word to each group.

6 Make adjectives from the letters. Then match the words with their definitions.

gyuhnr	wsol	efre
ads	hapce	snuorve

1 doesn't cost very much: _cheap_
2 how you feel before an exam: _nervouse_
3 not happy: _sad_
4 you want something to eat: _Hungry_
5 you don't pay for it: _free_
6 not fast: _slow_

Recycling Center

7 Complete the paragraph with these verbs:

ride	work	watch	live
get up	like	stay	enjoy

Terry Samuels [1] _lives_ in a yurt on an island in Washington State. His life is very simple. He [2] _____ when the sun rises and he [3] _____ on his small farm. He doesn't have a car, so he [4] _____ his bicycle everywhere, and he never [5] _____ television because he doesn't have electricity! Twice a year he sees his friends in Seattle. They [6] _____ the excitement of city life. But most of the time he [7] _____ at home. "It's a peaceful life," he says. "And I [8] _____ it here."

8 Fill in the blanks with *at*, *in*, or *on*.

1 _____at_____ a quarter to six
2 _____ September 25
3 _____ February
4 _____ noon

Fun Spot

Complete the crossword.

ACROSS →

(crossword grid)

Across

1 I don't write by hand, I use the __.
6 It's dark. Turn on the __.
7 What time does the bus __ for Nantucket?
8 Likes very much
9 You wash dishes in it.
11 When you're hungry you __.
12 You see the view from this.

Down

1 A person you work with
2 Many people like it—it's __.
3 You watch this at home.
4 She __ many books.
5 You sleep in these.
10 What's his name? —I don't __.

5 Public places

✔ Indoor places
✔ Present continuous

1 ▸ Listening

a Look at the pictures of the airport. Answer the questions.

1 Which pictures show these places?

a gate   customs   baggage claim

2 What do you think the problem is in each picture?

b **AUDIO** Listen. Write the letter of the picture for each conversation.

1 __   2 __   3 __

c **AUDIO** Listen again. List the five cities mentioned in the conversations.

1 *Hong Kong*
2 _____
3 _____
4 _____
5 _____

d **AUDIO** Match each sentence with a picture from 1a. Listen again if necessary.

1 It's snowing in Boston, and the airport is closed.   *B*
2 I'm looking for my suitcase.   __
3 He's traveling to Los Angeles.   __
4 They're putting some baggage from Mexico City over there.   __
5 We're putting people on flights to New York.   __
6 He's standing right here.   __

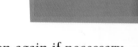

2 ▶ Focus on Grammar

a Look at 1d on page 27. When do you use the present continuous? Circle *a* or *b*.

   a For an action in progress **right now** or **around now**

   b For an action that happens **regularly**

Present continuous: Statements

Affirmative		Negative	
I **am**		I**'m not**	
You **are**		You **aren't**	
He / She / It **is**	**leaving** right now.	He / She / It **isn't**	**leaving** right now.
We **are**		We **aren't**	
They **are**		They **aren't**	

Spelling -ing endings

- For one syllable words ending in one vowel + a consonant, double the consonant: *putting, getting,* but *eating, opening*
- Drop *e* before *-ing*, but keep *y*: *having, taking,* but *studying*

---

b Complete the paragraph. Use the present continuous.

Tessa? Hi, it's Mike. Listen, I have bad news. The flight to Boston is canceled because ¹ *it's snowing*_____ (it / snow) in Boston. ²_____ (We / wait) in the airport. ³_____ (They / put) us on a flight to New York. So ⁴_____ (we / sit) at the gate right now. ⁵_____ (Sue / read) a book, and ⁶_____ (I / eat) a horrible sandwich…. Oh…wait a minute. I think ⁷_____ (they / call) our flight. Yes! ⁸_____ (It / leave) now. I'll call you later, OK?

c AUDIO Listen and check your answers.

d Look at the pictures. Find seven more differences. Use the present continuous.

Example *In picture A, a woman is looking at magazines. In B, she's looking at postcards.*

3 In Conversation

AUDIO Why is Jay at the mall? What about Nina?
Listen. Then read.

Jay:	Hello, Nina.
Nina:	Jay! How are you?
Jay:	I'm fine. Are you enjoying the music?
Nina:	Yes, it's very good. What are you doing here?
Jay:	I'm waiting for Cindy. She's buying a jacket. What about you?
Nina:	I'm shopping for a birthday present.

4 Focus on Grammar

▼ **Help Desk**

What are you doing here?
means *Why are you here?*

a Look at the chart. Underline two present continuous questions in the conversation above.

Present continuous: Questions

Questions	Answers
Are you enjoying the music?	Yes, **I am.** / No, **I'm not.**
What **are you doing**?	**I'm shopping** for a birthday present.
Is she enjoying the music?	Yes, **she is.** / No, **she isn't.**
What **is she doing**?	**She's shopping** for a birthday present.
Are they enjoying the music?	Yes, **they are.** / No, **they aren't.**
What **are they doing**?	**They're shopping** for a birthday present.

b **AUDIO** Write the questions in this conversation. Listen and check your answers.

Ruth: Hi, James!
<u>¹ *What are you doing here?*</u>
(What / you do / here)

James: We're celebrating my mother's birthday.

Ruth: ²_____?
(you / have / a good time)

James: Oh, yes.
³_____?
(Where / you / sit)

Ruth: Over there in the corner. I'm with my friend, Tom.

James: ⁴_____? (he / wear / a blue sweater)

Ruth: Yes, he is.

James: ⁵_____? (he / talk to / a woman in a red dress)

Ruth: What woman?

c Work with a partner. **A**, think of someone in the class. **B**, ask questions. Guess the person.

Examples *Is it a man or a woman? Is she sitting near / next to…? Is she wearing…?*

29

5 *KnowHow*: Pronunciation of *-ing* endings

a **AUDIO** Listen and repeat. Practice the pronunciation of the *-ing* endings.

What are you doing? —I'm enjoying the music.
What is she wearing? —She's wearing a dress.
Where are they sitting? —They're sitting over there.

b Work with a partner. Practice one of the conversations on page 29. Pay attention to the pronunciation of the *-ing* endings.

6 Speaking

Work with a partner. Discuss the questions about the pictures. Use your own ideas.

Who are these people?   Where are they?
What are they talking about?   What are they doing?

7 Writing

a Read the paragraph. Which picture in section 6 is the writer describing?

> I think these people are university or high school students. The boy is the boyfriend of one of the girls. They're sitting in a café, drinking water, and talking. I think they're talking about school work. Maybe they're doing homework together. They're speaking in sign language.

b Write a paragraph about one of the other pictures.

c Work with a partner. Compare your paragraphs. How are your interpretations different?

8 ▶ Language in Action: Directions

a Look at the picture and read the conversation. Fill in the missing word.

> **Mike:** Excuse me. I'm looking for the _____.
> **Sue:** They're on the second floor. Go straight up the escalator and turn left.
> **Mike:** Thank you.

b **AUDIO** Listen and check your answer.

c Look at the picture. Give directions to other places in the mall. Use the expressions in the box.

GIVING DIRECTIONS	
It's	right over there.
	straight ahead.
They're	on the left / right.
	on the second floor.
Go (straight) up / down	the corridor.
	the escalator.
Turn left / right.	

KEY

🚻 Restrooms	$ Cash Machine	ℂ Telephones
? Information Desk	P Parking Garage	🍴 Snack Bar

d Work with a partner. Give directions from your classroom to places like these:

the restrooms   a snack bar   a coffee shop   a public telephone

9 ▶ Vocabulary: Numbers

a **AUDIO** Listen and repeat the numbers.

76	seventy-six
876	eight hundred (and) seventy-six
5,876	five thousand, eight hundred (and) seventy-six
1,245,876	one million, two hundred forty-five thousand, eight hundred (and) seventy-six

b Work with a partner. Write six numbers. Dictate the numbers to your partner. Then compare the numbers on your papers. Are they the same?

10 ▸ Reading

a Which of these do you usually find in a mall?

department stores	a bank	a hotel	restaurants
movie theaters	a swimming pool	a post office	

b Read the article. Which of the places above are mentioned?

The World's Largest Mall

The West Edmonton Mall in Alberta, Canada is the biggest shopping and entertainment complex in the world. It attracts nine million tourists a year. They travel to Edmonton from all over just to shop. Many tourists never leave the mall during their visit to Edmonton. They stay in one of the two hotels in the complex.

With the help of a map, you can explore the mall for days. It covers more than 493,000 square meters (5.3 million square feet). It is the size of 48 city blocks, employs more than 23,000 people, and has parking for 20,000 cars. There are more than 800 shops and department stores and about 110 restaurants.

The mall is not just a place to shop and eat. The complex has 26 movie theaters and a giant amusement park. The weather gets cold in Edmonton, but even when it's freezing outside, you can swim in one of the indoor swimming pools at the World Waterpark. There is also a skating rink, and there is a miniature golf course in the complex.

All of this is available 365 days a year. So, what are you waiting for?

c Read the article again. Fill in the missing numbers. Then read the numbers aloud.

WEST EDMONTON MALL: STATISTICS

1 Total area: _493,000 m²_   **4** Employees: _____   **7** Restaurants: _____

2 Tourists every year: _____   **5** Parking spaces: _____   **8** Movie theaters: _____

3 Hotels: _____   **6** Stores: _____   **9** Days mall is open: _____

d Find a word in the article that means the following. (1) = paragraph number.

1 a group of buildings (1): _complex_   3 a place to go ice-skating (3): _____

2 very cold (3): _____   4 small (3): _____

e Work with a partner. Discuss the questions.

1 Why do you think the West Edmonton Mall is so popular?
2 Why do people like shopping malls?
3 How often do you go to shopping malls?

6 Now and then

✔ Time and daily schedules
✔ Simple past: Statements

1 ▶ Listening

a Work with a partner. Discuss the questions.

1 Would you like to have more time in your day?
2 What do you think "time management" is?

b **AUDIO** Listen to the first part of the talk about time management. Answer the questions.

1 What is "time management"?
2 Who is Robert?
3 What is Robert's problem?

c **AUDIO** Now listen to the rest of the talk. Why is the speaker talking about Robert?

d **AUDIO** Listen to the second part of the talk again. Fill in the missing times in Robert's journal.

Time Management, Inc.
Name: Robert Doherty
Journal for: Thursday, March 17

8:30	arrived at work / read and answered e-mail
____	checked the business news on the Internet
9:15	read the sports news
____	went to a coffee shop (waited ten minutes)
10:00	met Sue Porter / talked about her car problem
____	got back to the office / helped Jim with a new computer program
11:00	

e What do you think of Robert's use of time?

2 Focus on Grammar

a Look at the chart. Then underline the verbs in the past tense in Robert's journal on page 33.

Simple past: Statements			
Affirmative: Regular verbs	I You	**arrived** late **checked** the e-mail	yesterday. two days ago. last Thursday. on March 17th.
Affirmative: Irregular verbs	He She It	**met** a colleague **went** to a coffee shop **came** on time	
Negative: All verbs	We They	**didn't arrive** late **didn't meet** a colleague	

b Here are some common irregular past forms of verbs. What are the base forms?

1 went   _go_   5 made   _____   9 left   _____
2 had   _____   6 put   _____   10 came   _____
3 wrote   _____   7 bought _____   11 took   _____
4 gave   _____   8 ate   _____   12 got   _____

c Complete the paragraph with the verbs above.

Robert didn't ^{1} __go__ out for lunch. He ^{2} _bought_ a sandwich at the corner store and ^{3} _____ it at his desk. Then he ^{4} _____ a few phone calls. At 3:00 he ^{5} _____ the first paragraph of the weekly report, but he didn't ^{6} _____ time to finish it. A colleague ^{7} _____ to his office. She ^{8} _____ a problem with her computer. Robert ^{9} _____ her some advice. It ^{10} _____ a long time. At 5:00, Robert ^{11} _____ the report in his bag and ^{12} _____ the office. The traffic was terrible. He didn't ^{13} _____ home until 7:00.

3 KnowHow: Pronunciation of -ed endings

a **AUDIO** Listen to these sentences. How is the -ed ending pronounced? Check the boxes.

Examples *traveled* / d /, *checked* / t /, *celebrated* / ɪd /

	/ d /	/ t /	/ ɪd /
1 I arrived at work.	✓		
2 She helped him.			
3 We waited a long time.			
4 You finished it.			
5 They visited us.			
6 I answered the phone.			

b Now repeat the sentences. Practice the pronunciation of the -ed endings.

c Look back at Robert's time journal on page 33. Describe Robert's morning. Practice the pronunciation of the -ed endings.

Example *At 8:30, Robert arrived at work. He read and answered his e-mail.*

4 Vocabulary: Verbs and prepositions

a Alexandra Meli is a journalist in Milan, Italy. Read the description of her day. What did she do to save time?

Alexandra Meli, Journalist
Milan, Italy

JUST ANOTHER DAY IN MILAN, ITALY

I had a normal day yesterday. I woke up at 7:30, jumped into the shower, and dressed. As usual, I listened to the morning news at the same time. I didn't have breakfast. I'm never hungry in the mornings. I made two cups of strong, black coffee and worked for about three hours.

At noon, I realized I was late for an interview with an actor, so I drove like crazy to the TV station. I got to the TV station on time, but the actor didn't come. I ate a sandwich while I waited for him and talked to some other journalists about the events of the day.

Then I called my mother to say, "Happy birthday!" From there I got into my car and went to the office of the newspaper where I work. I arrived at the office at 1:45—late for a 1:30 meeting.

b Fill in the blanks with *at*, *to*, *for*, or *N*. (*N*=nothing) Check your answers by looking at the description above.

1 Alexandra listened ____to____ the news.
2 She got _____ the TV station on time.
3 She waited _____ the actor.
4 She talked _____ some other journalists.
5 She called _____ her mother.
6 She went _____ the newspaper office.
7 She arrived _____ the office late.

c Make true sentences about your day yesterday. Use some of the verbs and prepositions in 4b. Include negatives.

Example   *I didn't go to work. I went to the beach. I called a friend.*

5 Writing

a Make some notes about what you did this morning or yesterday morning. Then work with a partner and describe your morning.

b Write a description like the one in 4a. Title it: *Just Another Morning in…* (your city and country).

c Work in small groups. Read each other's paragraphs. Who had the busiest morning?

6 ▶ In Conversation

AUDIO Who thinks the "old days" were good—
Kelly or Paula? Listen. Then read.

Paula: Look at these old photographs, Kelly!
Those were the good old days.
Kelly: Do you really think so?
Paula: Yes. Life was simple, uncomplicated…
Kelly: Oh, come on! It wasn't so easy back then.
Paula: I know, but people had more time. They
weren't always in a hurry.
Kelly: But they had other problems. I prefer the
twenty-first century!

7 ▶ Focus on Grammar

a Look at the chart. Underline *was, wasn't, were,* and *weren't* in the conversation above.

Simple past: *be*		
I	**was / wasn't**	
You	**were / weren't**	in a hurry back then.
He / She	**was / wasn't**	
We / They	**were / weren't**	

b Complete the paragraph. Use *was, wasn't, were,* or *weren't.*

Yesterday, Kelly and I saw a great exhibit of photographs. It ¹ _was_ at the Fine Arts
Museum. It ² _____ early in the morning and there ³ _____ any other people at all,
so we ⁴ _____ alone. There ⁵ _____ about 50 photos in the exhibition. The photos
showed everyday life in the United States from the 19th century. It ⁶ _____ really
interesting. Of course, at that time there ⁷ _____ any television and there ⁸ _____
even electricity in some places. Everyday life ⁹ _____ very different!

8 ▶ Speaking

a Work in groups. Look at the photographs. Say how life was different in the past.

Example *People worked on the land. They didn't use computers. They weren't in a hurry.*

b Do you believe in "the good old days"? Why or why not?

9 ▶ Reading

a Work with a partner. Discuss the questions.

1 How did people tell time in the past?
2 How do you find out the exact time?

b Read the article. When and why were time zones established in the United States?

It's about time!

Nowadays the clock dominates our lives so much that it is hard to imagine life without it. Before industrialization, most societies used the sun or the moon to tell the time.

When mechanical clocks first appeared, they were immediately popular. It was fashionable to own a watch or a clock. People invented the expression "of the clock" or "o'clock" to refer to this new way to tell time.

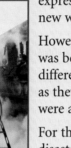

However, these early clocks were decorative, but not always useful. This was because towns, provinces, and even neighboring villages had different ways to tell time. Travelers had to reset their clocks repeatedly as they moved from one place to another. In the United States, there were about 70 different time zones as late as the 1860s.

For the growing network of railroads, the lack of time standards was a disaster. Often, stations just a few miles apart set their clocks at different times. There were frequently two clocks at each station: one for local time and the other for railroad time. Finally in 1883, the railroads established the four time zones used in the United States today.

c Read the article again. Circle the correct answer.

1 In the old days, people used __ to tell the time.
  a clocks   b societies   c nature
2 The first mechanical clocks were __.
  a popular and useful   b popular but not useful   c not popular
3 The railroads had a problem because __.
  a local time was different at each stop   b the trains moved backward and forward
  c there were two clocks at each station

d Find a word in the article that means the following. (2) = paragraph number.

1 made something for the first time (2):   _____
2 to change the time on a clock (3):   _____
3 a system of transportation (4):   _____
4 absence (4):   _____

e Work in groups. Compare your watches. Do you agree on the correct time?

10 ▶ Language in Action: Apologies

a AUDIO Listen and fill in the blanks. Is John angry with Molly?

Molly:	I'm sorry I'm late.
John:	¹_____?
Molly:	I was in a meeting at work, and it didn't finish until 6:00.
John:	²_____.

b Practice the conversation. Use different phrases from the chart below.

QUESTIONS	APOLOGIZING	ACCEPTING
What happened? Where were you?	I'm sorry I'm late.	Don't worry about it. That's OK.

c Work with a partner. Apologize for being late. Use the excuses below or your own ideas.

The traffic was terrible.	**I woke up late.**	**My watch stopped.**
The bus didn't come.	**I had a problem at work / school.**	

11 ▶ Speaking

a Look at the survey. When do you usually arrive for these things? Put checks (✔) in the appropriate boxes.

	On time	Up to 10 minutes late	10–30 minutes late	30–60 minutes late	More than 1 hour late
work					
a class					
a meeting with a friend					
a meeting at work					
dinner at someone's house					
a party at someone's house					

b Work in small groups. Compare your surveys. When is it important to be on time?

7 Food for thought

✔ Food and health
✔ Countable and uncountable nouns; expressions of quantity

1 ▷ Reading

a Work with a partner. Discuss the following:

   1 Where do you shop for food?
   2 Name some of the foods you buy.

b Read the advice about healthy food shopping. Check the items the writer recommends.

   1 fresh fruit and vegetables __   4 cookies and crackers __
   2 poultry (chicken, duck) __   5 candy __
   3 eggs __   6 dried fruit __

SHOP SMART in the Supermarket

Six steps to healthy food shopping

Suggestions from our food writer of the month

- Shop the edges of the supermarket. Most supermarkets put healthy food on the sides of the store: fruit, vegetables, meat, poultry, and fish.

- Your shopping cart should look colorful. Carrots, peppers, tomatoes, oranges, and broccoli add color to your shopping cart—and health to your diet.

- Red meat is OK. But fish, chicken, beans, and eggs are also excellent sources of protein.

- Don't buy food your great-great-grandfather could not recognize—food that did not exist a hundred years ago. Some packaged foods, like cookies and crackers, have a lot of artificial ingredients. Read the labels. If you can't pronounce most of the ingredients on the package, don't buy it!

- The labels "low fat" and "sugar free" do not necessarily mean "good for your health."

- Don't go shopping when you are hungry. You will buy more unnecessary snacks. If you have a sweet tooth, buy dried fruit instead of candy or cookies.

FOOD   92

c Work with a partner. Look at the article again. Explain each piece of advice.

   1 Shop the edges of the supermarket.
   2 Your shopping cart should look colorful.
   3 Don't buy food that your great-great-grandfather could not recognize.
   4 If you can't pronounce most of the ingredients on the package, don't buy it.
   5 Don't go shopping when you're hungry.

d Do you agree or disagree with this advice? Which piece of advice is the most useful?

2 Vocabulary: Food

a Work with a partner. Complete the words for items 1–10. (All the items are in the article on page 39.)

1 _be_____
2 _ca_____
3 _pe_____
4 _br_____
5 _to_____
6 _or_____
7 _eg_____
8 _ca_____
9 _cr_____
10 _co_____

b Divide the words above into these categories.

Uncountable nouns (singular)	Countable nouns (singular or plural)
candy	beans
broccoli	carrots

▼ **Help Desk**

Some words that are uncountable, like *coffee* or *soda*, are sometimes used in the plural.

Can I have three coffees, please? (= three cups of coffee)

c **AUDIO** Complete the expressions with words from the list. Then listen and check your answers.

mineral water	fruit	juice	soup	milk
cereal	soda	bread	pizza	cheese

1 a slice of _bread, cheese, pizza_

2 a glass of _____

3 a bowl of _____

4 a can of _____

3 KnowHow: Dictionary tips

a Look at the dictionary extract below. Identify the following information:

grammar   meaning   pronunciation

b Answer the questions.

1 Where is the stress on the word *apple*? How do you know?
2 What do you think [C] means?

apple /ˈæpl/ *noun* [C] a hard, round fruit with smooth green, red or yellow skin: *an apple tree* ○ *apple juice*

1 _____ 2 _____ 3 _____

c Use a dictionary to look up one or more words on this page.

4 Listening

a What kinds of food do you think are in the following diets?

a traditional American diet   a traditional Mediterranean diet
a traditional Asian diet

b **AUDIO** Listen to the interview. Which diet does the doctor prefer?

c **AUDIO** Listen again. Check the features of each diet that the doctor mentions.

Traditional diet	Butter	Fish	Fruit or vegetables	Salt	Desserts or sugar
American					
Mediterranean					
Asian					

d What is a traditional diet where you live?

5 Focus on Grammar

a Look at the chart and circle the correct answers.

1 Use *much* before (countable / uncountable) nouns.
2 Use *many* before (countable / uncountable) nouns.
3 Use *some* in (affirmative / negative) sentences.
4 Use *any* in (affirmative / negative) sentences.

How much / many...?; some, any, a lot of, not much / many

Uncountable nouns		Countable nouns	
How much fruit do you eat?		**How many** vegetables do you eat?	
Short answer	*Long answer*	*Short answer*	*Long answer*
A lot.	I eat **a lot** of fruit.	**A lot.**	I eat **a lot** of vegetables.
Not much.	I **don't** eat **much** fruit.	**Not many.**	I don't eat **many** vegetables.
Some.	I eat **some** fruit.	**Some.**	I eat **some** vegetables.
Not any.	I **don't** eat **any** fruit.	**Not any.**	I don't eat **any** vegetables.

---

b Fill in the blanks with *some, any, much,* or *many*.

1 How _____ water do you drink every day?
2 I can't eat _____ cheese. I'm allergic.
3 How _____ slices of pizza did you eat?
4 I'd like _____ coffee, please.
5 Children, please don't eat so _____ cookies!
6 I didn't eat _____ breakfast: just a slice of toast.

c Work with a partner. Talk about how much of the following you usually eat or drink.

seafood   dessert   eggs   coffee   juice   soda   snacks   fast food

6 ▷ Writing

a Read the e-mail. Who do you think it is from?

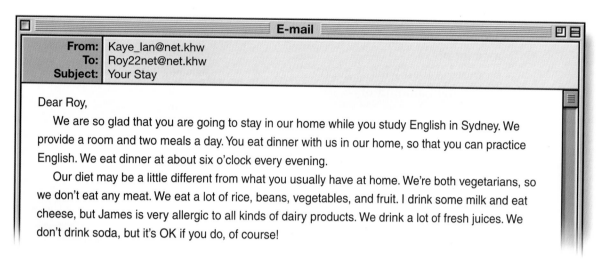

```
┌─────────────────────────────────────────────────────────────────┐
│ □                        E-mail                              回▤ │
├─────────────────────────────────────────────────────────────────┤
│    From: │ Kaye_Ian@net.khw                                       │
│      To: │ Roy22net@net.khw                                       │
│ Subject: │ Your Stay                                              │
├─────────────────────────────────────────────────────────────────┤
```

Dear Roy,

   We are so glad that you are going to stay in our home while you study English in Sydney. We provide a room and two meals a day. You eat dinner with us in our home, so that you can practice English. We eat dinner at about six o'clock every evening.

   Our diet may be a little different from what you usually have at home. We're both vegetarians, so we don't eat any meat. We eat a lot of rice, beans, vegetables, and fruit. I drink some milk and eat cheese, but James is very allergic to all kinds of dairy products. We drink a lot of fresh juices. We don't drink soda, but it's OK if you do, of course!

b Work with a partner. Compare your eating habits to those of the people in the e-mail.

c Imagine that a student from another country is coming to stay at your house. Write a note to this person about your eating habits. Include information about:

what time you eat   what you usually eat   what you usually drink

7 ▷ Reading

a Look at the headline and photograph. What do you think a couch potato is?

b Read the article and answer the questions.

1 How does this machine work?
2 Why do people use it?
3 Who is David Allison and what does he believe?

c What ways can you think of to encourage people to exercise?

No More Couch Potatoes!

Here's a way for parents to move their snack-eating, TV-watching children from the family sofa: a bicycle connected electrically to the TV. To see their favorite shows, the kids have to pedal.

About 55 percent of American adults and more than 13 percent of young people ages 6 through 17 are overweight. Research shows that young people are watching too much television and eating too many snacks at the same time. Many of them are not getting enough exercise. Formal exercise programs do not help much because it is difficult to get to a gym or playground regularly, particularly for young children with working parents.

As a result, scientists are looking for home-based ways to get kids moving. David Allison, the inventor of the "TV-cycle", believes that scientists should look for imaginative ways to encourage physical activity. He also suggests charging money to ride an elevator. This way, more people will use the stairs!

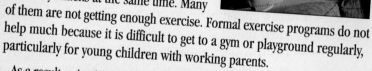

Tests show patients improve

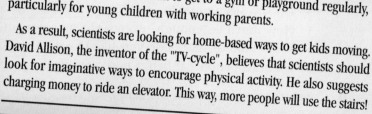

Focus on Grammar

a Look at the chart and the sentences from the reading. Answer the questions.

1 *Too much* and *too many* mean:
  a a lot of
  b more… than what is good
  c the right amount of
2 *Enough* means:
  a a lot of
  b more… than what is good
  c the right amount of

…and …… …pere… …or young… …ple ages 6 through 17 are overweight. Research shows that young people are watching too much television and eating too many snacks at the same time. Many of them are not getting enough exercise. Fc help much because it is difficult to get tc

Too much, too many; (not) enough

Uncountable nouns	Countable nouns
A lot of people watch **too much television**. Do you get **enough exercise**?	They eat **too many snacks**. There are**n't enough playgrounds**.

b Look at the statistics. Then circle the correct answers.

DIET AND HEALTH HABITS OF AVERAGE ADULTS IN THE U.S.

Never eat breakfast	44%
Sleep 6 hours or less	22%
Don't exercise regularly	59%
Eat snacks every day	75%
Hours spent watching TV (per week)	31

Statistics show that a lot of people in the United States don't eat [1](any / enough) breakfast, and many people don't get [2](any / enough) sleep. As a result, they [3](have / don't have) enough energy for the day, and they eat [4](too many / enough) snacks. Fifty-nine percent of the population doesn't get [5](any / enough) regular exercise. And everyone spends [6](enough / too much) time in front of the TV!

c **AUDIO** Listen and check your answers.

Speaking

a Work in small groups. Discuss the questions.

1 How much time do you spend watching TV?
2 How much sleep do you need?
3 Do you sleep more or less than you did a year ago? Five years ago?
4 How much is "enough" exercise? Can a person get too much exercise?
5 What kind of snacks do you like to eat? Are all snacks bad?
6 Do most people eat better now than in the past?

b Compare your ideas with the class.

10 ▶ Language in Action: Restaurant talk

a **AUDIO** Put the conversation in order. Then listen and check your answers.

— Does that come with vegetables?

— Yes, of course.

— Salmon, OK.

_1_ Are you ready to order?

— That sounds good.

— Would you like something to drink?

— Yes, please. I'll have the salmon.

— Yes. Could I have some mineral water, please?

— It comes with potatoes and a small salad.

b Work with a partner. Practice the conversation.

c Work in small groups. You are in a restaurant. Read the menu and order a meal.

> **ORDERING**
> - Would you like…?
> - I'll have….
> - I'd like….
> - Could I have…?
> - Can I have…?
> - Does that come with …?

MENU

Starters

Deep Fried Chicken Wings
with hot and spicy sauce — $4.50

Mushrooms in Garlic Sauce — $3.95

Broccoli and Cheese Soup — $3.50

House Salad
lettuce, carrots, tomatoes, and choice of dressing — $3.75

Entrees

Hamburger
served with French fries and a small salad — $7.75

Poached Salmon
in lemon pepper sauce — $11.95

Roast Chicken
breast of chicken in garlic sauce, served over rice — $10.95

Vegetarian Pasta
a variety of vegetables and mushrooms in a creamy sauce — $8.50

Desserts

Apple Pie — $3.95

Ice Cream
chocolate, banana, or strawberry — $2.75

Cheesecake
served with strawberries — $4.50

11 ▶ Speaking

a Work with a partner. Create your own menu. Fill in the blanks with your own ideas.

b Exchange menus with another pair and take turns ordering meals.

MENU

Starters

Entrees

Desserts

8 Read all about it

✔ News and events
✔ Simple past: Questions; *could / couldn't*

1 ▶ In Conversation

AUDIO Look at the headline. When and where did this happen? Listen. Then read.

Adam: Did you hear about that guy? He spent three days in a block of ice.
Patty: That's incredible. Why did he do it?
Adam: He wanted to break a world record.
Patty: Was he OK?
Adam: I think so. He got out yesterday.
Patty: Where was that?
Adam: Right here in New York. In Times Square.
Patty: Amazing!

Man Spends 3 Days in Ice

2 ▶ Vocabulary: Describing events

a Add these words to the chart. Some words can go in more than one column.

weird   awful   scary   amazing   great   incredible   terrible   wonderful

Strange	Bad	Good	Surprising	Frightening
weird	awful			scary

b Work with a partner. Read the headlines aloud. Respond using some of the words above.

Example   A: *Listen to this. "Woman finds missing dog—three years later."*
              B: *That's amazing.*

Woman Finds Missing Dog — Three Years Later

House Prices Are Going Down

Young People Smoke More Than Ever

Rich People Not Always Happy, Survey Finds

3 ▶ Focus on Grammar

a Look at the chart. Fill in the blanks below.

1 Use _____ or *were* to form questions in the past with *be*.
2 Use _____ to form questions in the past with other verbs.

Simple past: Questions and answers		
be		
When	**Was** he OK? **was** it?	Yes, he **was**. / No, he **wasn't**. Yesterday.
Where	**Were** you there? **were** you yesterday?	Yes, we **were**. / No, we **weren't**. We **were** at work.
Regular and irregular verbs		
What	**Did** you **read** the news? **did** he **do**?	Yes, I **did**. / No, I **didn't**. He **broke** the record.

b Fill in the blanks with *Did, Was,* or *Were*.

1 _____ you at school yesterday?
2 _____ you hear the news?
3 _____ something happen?
4 _____ you at home last night?
5 _____ you watch TV?
6 _____ it interesting?

c AUDIO Look at the headline. Make complete questions using *did, was,* or *were*. Then listen and fill in the answers.

▼ *Help Desk*

Newspaper headlines often use the simple present to describe past events.

MAN SWIMS ACROSS THE ATLANTIC

A French swimmer arrived back in France yesterday after swimming there–all the way from the United States. Benoît Lecomte

1 Where / this? *Where was this?* *France*
2 Where / the man swim from?
3 How long / trip?
4 How many hours a day / swim?
5 Where / sleep?
6 How much money / raise?

4 Reading

a Read the headline and look at the picture. What do you want to know about this story? Write two questions.

b Read the story. Does it answer your questions?

○ E V E N I N G   E D I T I O N

Squirrel helps police find stolen goods

POLICE OFFICERS INVESTIGATING A BURGLARY yesterday were amazed when a squirrel helped them find the stolen goods. The bushy-tailed detective led them right to the place where the goods were.

In the early hours of the morning, police arrested a man for breaking into a garage and stealing items in Bath, England. Later in the morning, they came back to the garage to look for the stolen goods, and they found a squirrel in front of the garage.

The animal ran away but then stopped and looked at the officers as if to say, "Come with me." So the police followed. The squirrel led them all the way around the block—a distance of about 150 yards, looking back often to check that the officers were behind it. Then it just ran up a tree and sat on a branch and waited for them.

When the police officers got there, they found all of the stolen goods from the burglary behind the tree. The squirrel left quickly and did not stay to accept a reward.

c Answer the questions.

1 Why did the police arrest a man?
2 Why did they go back to the garage?
3 Why did the police follow the squirrel?
4 Where were the stolen goods?

d What do you think of the story?

5 *KnowHow*: Vocabulary through reading

a Underline these words in the article above.

   breaking into   yards   a branch   a reward

b Choose the correct definition for each word. Then write expressions from the article that helped you.

1 *breaking into* means ((entering a building by force) / crashing a car into something) How do you know? *The man stole things; the police came; it was late at night*

2 a *yard* is (a path in front of a house / a measurement of length)
   How do you know? _____

3 a *branch* is probably (a type of wall / part of a tree)
   How do you know? _____

4 a *reward* is (something that you get in return for work or for helping someone / a type of food you eat for breakfast)
   How do you know? _____

c Write your own sentences with the words in 8b.

6 ▶ In Conversation

AUDIO What happened to Jill? Listen. Then read.

Jill: Jerry, did I tell you about the time I nearly drowned?

Jerry: No. When was that?

Jill: Oh, a long time ago. I was at the beach with some friends. I went swimming, and I went out too far. I couldn't swim back.

Jerry: So what did you do?

Jill: I yelled to my friends, but they couldn't hear me.

Jerry: So how did you get out?

Jill: Well, they finally realized I was in trouble. They swam in and pulled me out.

Jerry: Hey, that's scary.

Jill: It sure was! After that, I learned to be careful.

7 ▶ Focus on Grammar

a Underline two sentences with *couldn't* in the conversation above. Circle the correct answer.

Couldn't is the past form of (aren't / can't / won't).

Could / couldn't		
Statements		
I / You He / She / It We / They	**could / couldn't**	swim.
Questions	**Answers**	
Could Jill swim? **Could** her friends hear her?	Yes, she **could**. Yes, they **could**.	No, she **couldn't**. No, they **couldn't**.

b Choose *could / couldn't* and the correct ending for each sentence.

1 My mother took the car because my father		believe it.
2 We were very surprised. We		see much better.
3 When I got my new glasses, I	could	find it.
4 Martha looked everywhere for her sweater, but she	couldn't	get down.
5 The cat climbed up the tree, but it		drive.

c Work with a partner. Think of a time when you were in danger or saw someone else in danger. Describe what happened.

48

Language in Action: Narration

a Look at pictures 1–3.

    1 Identify the following:

        antique store   **salesperson**   **vase**

    2 What is happening in each picture?

b **AUDIO** Listen. Answer the questions.

    1 Why did George go into the store?
    2 What happened when he went to pay for the vase?

c **AUDIO** Listen again. Check the expressions that you hear.

BEGINNING	SEQUENCING	
__ One day…	__ Then…	__ After a while…
	__ After that…	__ Finally…

d Work with a partner. Tell George's story using the expressions in the chart.

    Example   *One day, George went to an antique store because…*

Speaking

a Work with a partner. Tell the rest of George's story. Use the words and expressions below to help you.

open the door	locked	people outside	surprised
the sign	laughed	came back	went to sleep

b Work with a new partner. Tell the whole story from the beginning.

10 ▶ Writing

Write the story on page 49. Begin like this:

George loves to go to antique stores. One day...

11 ▶ Listening: Song

a Look at the picture below. What do you think is happening?

b Try to put the phrases in the correct place in the song.

arms around your waist   let me in   rang your bell   passed your house   tears in my eyes
"You're on the wrong block"   two silhouettes on the shade

SILHOUETTES

Took a walk and ¹_____ late last night
All the shades were pulled and drawn way down tight
From within, a dim light cast ²_____
Oh what a lovely couple they made

Put his ³_____, held you tight
Kisses I could almost taste in the night
Wondered why I'm not the guy whose silhouette's on the shade
I couldn't hide the ⁴_____

Lost control and ⁵_____, I was sore
" ⁶_____ or else I'll beat down your door"
When two strangers who have been two silhouettes on the shade
Said to my shock, ⁷_____

Rushed round to your house with wings on my feet
Loved you like I'd never loved you my sweet
Vowed that you and I would be two silhouettes on the shade
All of our days, two silhouettes on the shade

Glossary

shades = window coverings that you pull down

cast = to cause a shadow to appear

sore = angry

beat down your door = open your door by force

c **AUDIO** Now listen and check your answers.

d Work with a partner. Answer the questions.

1 What mistake did the man singing the song make?
2 What did he do when he realized his mistake?
3 Have you ever made a similar mistake?

e **AUDIO** Listen again and sing along if you want to. Then tell the story as if it happened to you.

Example *I took a walk and...*

▼ Help Desk

Sometimes in songs the subject is not in the sentence.

Took a walk and passed your house = I took a walk and passed your house.

Put his arms around your waist = He put his arms around your waist.

Units 5–8 Review

Grammar

1 Read the text. Who was David waiting for?

On Sunday, David went to the Portland airport to meet his friend Sarah. The arrival time of her flight from Denver was 7:20. He waited for the flight at gate 32 for thirty minutes. The flight arrived on time. David watched the people get off, but Sarah wasn't there. David talked to a woman at the information desk, but she couldn't tell him who was on the flight. He looked for Sarah in the baggage claim area, but she wasn't there either. He went home and called Sarah in Denver. "Oh no!" Sarah said. "You have the wrong day! My flight to Portland is tomorrow!"

2 Ask and answer questions about David. Use the information from the text above.

1 When _did David go to meet_ (go to meet) his friend Sarah?
He went on Sunday evening.

2 How long _____ (wait) for the flight?
_____

3 Who _____ (talk to) at the airport?
_____

4 Where _____ (look) for Sarah?
_____

5 What _____ (do) at home?
_____

3 Sarah is talking to a friend on the telephone. Complete the conversation using the simple present or present continuous.

Li: Hi, Sarah. How ¹ _are you_ ? (you / be)
Sarah: ² _____ (I / be) fine. And you?
Li: Just fine. What ³ _____ (you / do) right now?
Sarah: ⁴ _____ (I / pack) my bags for my trip to Portland.
Li: ⁵ _____?(you / go / Portland / often)
Sarah: Yes, I do.
Li: Is someone there with you? I can hear voices.
Sarah: ⁶ _____ (I / watch) television. I want to see what the weather's like there.
Li: What do they say?
Sarah: ⁷ _____ (It / rain) there right now. Actually, ⁸ _____ (it / rain) every time I go there.

4 Complete Sarah's diary with the irregular past tenses.

Monday—on my flight to Portland.
Esther ¹ _____ (come) to say goodbye at about 2:00. I only ² _____ (have) half an hour to get ready, so I ran around like crazy. I ³ _____ (write) a note to the landlord about the broken window, then I ⁴ _____ (put) everything in my bag and I ⁵ _____ (leave) the house. Of course I ⁶ _____ (can) not find a taxi, so I ⁷ _____ (take) the bus to the airport. I ⁸ _____ (buy) magazines to read before the flight left. I ⁹ _____ (get) on the plane at 5:00. It's now 6:10, so I'll be there soon.

5 Complete the sentences with your own ideas.

1 I don't have much _____.
2 My _____ has too many _____.
3 There aren't enough _____ in _____.
4 I need to buy some _____, but I don't need any _____.
5 I don't have many _____.

Vocabulary

6 ▶ Fill in the blanks with *to*, *at*, *for*, or *N*. (*N=nothing*)

1 Eva went _____ Canada last spring.
2 The flight arrived _____ the airport two hours late.
3 I usually listen _____ the radio to relax.
4 She waited _____ the bus for 40 minutes.
5 You should talk _____ Jack about the problem.
6 Sandy called _____ us on the phone yesterday.

7 ▶ Put the words into the correct groups. How many more words can you add?

cheese	amazing	bowl	shopping mall
weird	meat	lettuce	terrible
milk	pasta	cup	information desk
pizza	coffee	glass	scary

Food or drink	cheese
Public places	
Containers	
Adjectives	

Fun Spot

Use the clues to write the words in the horizontal spaces. The vertical word (highlighted) means "very cold."

1 "How are you?" "I'm _____."
2 You can make a sandwich using this basic food.
3 The flight is leaving from _____ number 62.
4 You use this to talk to people.
5 "He lived in a tree for 3 months." "That's _____!"
6 Very scary
7 She almost died because she couldn't swim. She almost _____.
8 "Don't go to the left, go to the _____."

Recycling Center

8 ▶ Circle the correct modal verb.

1 (Would / Can) you like some coffee?
2 I (should / can) fly a plane—I learned when I was twenty.
3 You (shouldn't / couldn't) talk like that about other people!
4 (Can / Would) I have a piece of pie?
5 Yoko doesn't like to go on boats because she (wouldn't / can't) swim.
6 (Should / Would) you like to go to the movies?
7 Your job sounds pretty bad. You (would / should) look for another one.

9 ▶ Complete the paragraph with words from the list.

snows	rainy	yellow	blue
cold	summer	green	red
fall	sunny		

I live in Quebec, Canada. It's a nice place to live because the weather is always different. We have four seasons—fall, winter, spring and ^{1}_____. In the winter, there is a lot of snow, and it's very ^{2}_____. Spring is warm, but sometimes it's ^{3}_____ and foggy. Summer is my favorite season because it's ^{4}_____. All of the trees are ^{5}_____, and the sky is ^{6}_____. In the ^{7}_____, the trees turn beautiful colors—mostly ^{8}_____ and ^{9}_____. The summer is short, and soon it's winter again and it ^{10}_____!

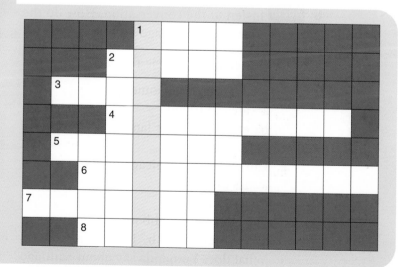

9 Cities and sites

✔ Descriptions of places
✔ Comparative and superlative adjectives

1 ▶ Vocabulary: Describing places

a Work with a partner. Put the words into the three categories below. Then compare answers with another pair.

beautiful	relaxing	cheap	warm
dangerous	dirty	exciting	expensive
large	modern	noisy	old
quiet	safe	small	cold

Usually good	Usually bad	Good or bad
beautiful	dangerous	large

Chicago, U.S.

b Look at the pictures of Chicago, U.S., and Santiago, Chile. Use some of the words in the box to describe each city.

Example   *Chicago and Santiago are beautiful.*
          Santiago is warm…

c Which words would you use to describe the place where you live?

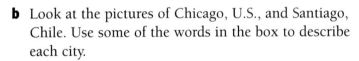

Santiago, Chile

2 ▶ Listening

a Look at the picture. Who do you think the people are?

b **AUDIO** Listen to the conversation. How do the women feel about Chicago and Santiago?

c **AUDIO** Listen again. Circle the correct answer.

1 Joe and the two women ___.
   a are old friends
   b are in the same family
   c just met
2 Christina likes Chicago because ___.
   a it's exciting   b it's big
   c it's safe
3 She likes her neighborhood because ___.
   a it's friendly   b it's in a safe area   c it's near her job
4 What does Fernanda say about Santiago?
   a It's big.   b It's quiet.   c It's her home.

Christina   Fernanda

3 ▷ Focus on Grammar

a Look at the chart and answer the questions.

1 How do you form the comparative of…

adjectives with one syllable?   adjectives with two or more syllables?

2 Which comparative forms are irregular?

Comparative adjectives	
Adjectives with one syllable	
Most adjectives: add -er Ending in consonant + vowel + consonant: Double the consonant and add -er Ending in -e: Add -r	Santiago is warm**er** than Chicago in February. Egypt is big**ger** than Kenya. His house is larg**er** than my house.
Adjectives with two or more syllables	
Ending in -y, change -y to -i and add -er Most others: Use *more*	Cities are nois**ier** than small towns. Small towns are **more** relaxing than big cities.
Irregular forms	
good better bad worse	Warm weather is **better** than cold weather.

b Write the comparative forms of these adjectives.

1 small   _____   6 hot   _____
2 beautiful   _____   7 dirty   _____
3 exciting   _____   8 noisy   _____
4 modern   _____   9 cheap   _____
5 safe   _____   10 high   _____

c **AUDIO** How much do you know? Work with a partner. Write sentences comparing the cities, using the adjectives in parentheses. Then listen and check your answers.

1 Sydney / Tokyo (large)   *Tokyo is larger than Sydney.*
2 Mexico City / Amsterdam (high)   _____
3 London / San Francisco (small)   _____
4 Dallas / Rome (modern)   _____
5 São Paulo / Bangkok (big)   _____
6 Moscow / Miami (cold)   _____

d Compare your city to other places that you know. Try to use all the comparative forms in 3c.

> ▼ **Help Desk**
>
> Be careful with word order!
>
> *Milan is more modern than Rome.*
>
> (Not: ~~Is more modern Milan than Rome.~~)

4 Language in Action: Opinions

a AUDIO What does Philip think? Does Wendy agree? Listen. Then read.

Wendy: Did you hear that Susan moved to Bali?
Philip: Bali! Wow! How did that happen?
Wendy: She went there on vacation and really liked it. She lives there now and works in a hotel.
Philip: Lucky her!
Wendy: Hmm… . I'm not so sure. I think it's hard to live in another country.
Philip: Really?
Wendy: Well, she doesn't speak the language very well.
Philip: That's true.
Wendy: Also, she's very far away from her friends and family.
Philip: Hmm… . Maybe you're right.

b AUDIO Look at the chart. Listen again. Check the expressions that Philip and Wendy use.

GIVING AN OPINION	AGREEING	DISAGREEING
__ I (don't) think…	__ I agree.	__ I disagree.
__ In my opinion…	__ (Maybe) you're right.	__ I'm not so sure.
__ If you ask me…	__ That's true.	__ I don't think so.

c Practice the conversation in 4a. Substitute different expressions from the chart above.

5 Speaking

a Read the following statements. Check whether you generally agree or disagree.

	Agree	Disagree
1 It's better to live in a house than an apartment.		
2 It's more relaxing to live in the country than in the city.		
3 It's more fun to be single than to be married.		
4 It's better to get married and have children when you're young.		
5 It's better to stay in your home town than to move away.		

b Work in small groups. Discuss the statements above. Say whether you agree or disagree, and why.

6 ▶ Reading

a Look at the statements. Which ones do you think are true?

1 People in warm climates are generally happier than people in cold climates. ___
2 People who live in the country are usually happier than people in the city. ___
3 People who live near their families are often happier than people who do not. ___

b Read the article. Write T (true) or F (false) next to each of the statements above, according to the information in the article.

Survey Finds The Happiest Places

Copenhagen, Denmark

What is the happiest place on earth? It's Denmark. A leading researcher has analyzed the results of years of surveys about happiness. The surveys asked thousands of people in more than 20 nations, "How happy are you?" Here are some conclusions.

Climate has little effect on happiness. People in warm Mediterranean countries, such as Portugal and Greece, often said they were unhappy. More people in Northern European countries—Denmark, the Netherlands, and Norway—said they were happy, even though their weather is probably the worst in Europe. It's cloudy in the summer and cold and dark in the winter.

Americans shouldn't move to the East or West

Coast to look for the good life. People in New York and California were not happier than people in other regions. In fact, the happiest parts of the United States are areas that are rural and traditionally poorer than other areas.

Psychologist Michael Hagerty says this is because people in rural areas tend to stay in the place where they grew up, near family and friends. People who have close ties to friends and family are usually happier than those who do not.

The conclusion? You don't need to move to Denmark to be happy. Hagerty says, "The best thing you can do to be happy is to develop good ties with friends and family. You can do that wherever you are, right now."

c Circle the correct answer for each sentence.

According to the article:

1 The research on happiness is based on ___.
a one survey   b more than one survey

2 People in Denmark, the Netherlands, and Norway were ___ than people in the rest of Europe.
a happier   b unhappier

3 Many Americans move to the East or West Coast ___.
a to look for a better life   b to be close to family and friends

4 According to the researchers, if you want to be happy, you should ___.
a move to a sunny place   b be close to your family and friends

d Find a word that means the same as the following. (1) = paragraph number.

1 weather (2): _____   3 in the country, not the city (3): _____
2 areas (3): _____   4 connections (4): _____

e Do you agree with the conclusions of the survey?

Focus on Grammar

a Look at the chart. Then underline the superlative forms in the article on page 56.

Superlative adjectives		
Adjectives with one syllable		
Add *-est* or *-st* (Follow the rules for comparative adjectives.)	the big**gest** the saf**est** the warm**est**	
Adjectives with two or more syllables		
Ending in *-y*, change *-y* to *-i* and add *-est* Most others: Use *most*	I live on the nois**iest** street in the city. What is the **most** interesting city in the world?	
Irregular forms		
good the best bad the worst	Which city has **the worst** winters on the East Coast?	
Note: Use *the* with superlative adjectives.		

b Fill in the blanks with the superlative form of the adjectives in parentheses.

1 *The best*__ (good) vacation I ever had was in Phuket, Thailand. We stayed in a hotel next to _____ (beautiful) beach on the island. We met some of _____ (friendly) people in the world.

2 _____ (interesting) place I ever visited was London. Unfortunately, I went in July— that's _____ (expensive) time to go to Europe. It's also _____ (busy) time of year there.

3 _____ (good) thing about my city is the weather. It's always sunny and warm. _____ (bad) thing is the noise. I live in _____ (old) part of the city, and there's a lot of traffic there.

c Find and correct six more mistakes in Joe's paragraph.

> Sightseeing
>
> *Joe, could you please make corrections here? Thanks, M.*
>
> *the most convenient place*
>
> The area near Central Square is ~~the place most convenient~~ for shopping and sightseeing. It is oldest part of the city, and it has the architecture most interesting. It is the more popular tourist area. There are many shops and restaurants, and some of the fashionable boutiques in the city. A best time to go is in the evening, when you can enjoy a meal at the City Café. This is the older restaurant in the area.

d Work with a partner. Discuss the questions.

1 When and where was your best vacation?
2 What is the most interesting place that you ever visited?
3 What are the best and worst things about where you live?

▼ Help Desk

Be careful with word order!

It is the most interesting city in the world.

(Not: *It is the city most interesting in the world.*)

8 ▸ *KnowHow*: **Word stress**

a AUDIO Listen to these words. Pay attention to the stressed syllables. Repeat the words.

a comfortable hotel   a convenient location   traditional food

b AUDIO Now listen to these words. Mark the stressed syllable in each word. Repeat the words.

1 a relaxing atmosphere	3 fashionable boutiques	5 popular cities
2 spectacular scenery	4 unusual festivals	6 expensive restaurants

c Which of the items above do you enjoy when you go on vacation?

9 ▸ Writing

a Read the paragraphs and write the titles. Choose from the list below.

The Best Roller Coaster Ride   The Most Unusual Place to Sleep   The Strangest Festival

Adventure Destinations Around the World

1 _____

Every August in Buñol, Spain, you can take part in "La Tomatina," the world's largest food fight. Tourists come from miles around and locals throw 240,000 pounds of tomatoes at them.

2 _____

The Steel Dragon 2000 in Nagashima, Japan, is 320 feet at its highest point. Trains run at 95 miles per hour. The ride takes about three minutes.

3 _____

The Hotel de Sal Playa in Bolivia is entirely made of salt. The walls are made of salt blocks stuck together with a mixture of salt and water. During the rainy season the owners replace damaged blocks with new ones. Even some of the furniture is made of salt!

b Work with a partner. Choose three of the following, or use your own ideas. Make a chart for your city or your country.

most spectacular scenery	most popular night spot	most interesting festival
most fashionable restaurant	friendliest people	best hotel

	Where?	Why?
Most spectacular scenery:	Copper Canyon	Big canyon with beautiful rock formations

c You are preparing a brochure for travelers to your country. Write a short paragraph about each of the places in your chart.

d Work in small groups. Exchange paragraphs. Compare your choices.

10 *On the job*

✔ Work and occupations
✔ *Have / has to; would rather, would prefer to*

▌ Reading

a Work with a partner. Look at the picture in the article. Which words would you use to describe the man's job?

> boring   dangerous   interesting   relaxing   unusual   stressful

b Read the article and answer the questions.

1 What is difficult about the job?
2 What does the painter like about his job?

A Head for HEIGHTS

When I tell people that I paint the Golden Gate Bridge, they think I start at one end, paint to the other end, and then start again. But that's not true. We're always painting the bridge, but we have to go where the paint is in bad condition. It's a dangerous job. You have to be careful all the time. You can't work up here without safety equipment. And the weather! It gets cold up here. Sometimes it's so cold, there's ice on the bridge. You have to wear warm clothes. Sometimes it's windy and foggy. On foggy days, you can't see anything. Other times, you're above the fog. Down below, tourists are shivering, and we're up here in T-shirts.

The view from the top is the thing I love about the job. On a sunny day like today, you can see from the ocean to the bay and all the way to the mountains. Of course, you have to have a head for heights!

c Read the article again. Answer these questions.

1 What different kinds of weather does the painter mention?
2 Look at the last sentence. What does *have a head for heights* mean?
   a be tall   b feel comfortable in high places

> ### ▼ Help Desk
>
> *You* in this sentence is impersonal. It means "a person."
>
> ***You** have to be careful.*
> = *A person* has to be careful.

2 Focus on Grammar

a Underline sentences with *have to* in the article on page 59. Then look at the chart and circle the correct answers below.

1 If you *have to do* something, it is (necessary / difficult).
2 If you *don't have to do* something, it is (impossible / unnecessary).

Have / has to		
I / You We / They	**have to** **don't have to**	
He / She	**has to** **doesn't have to**	work.

Note: *Don't have to* is not the same as *can't.*
They **don't have to** have special training. – not necessary
They **can't** work without safety equipment. – not permitted

b Complete the paragraph. Use *have to, has to, doesn't have to,* or *can't.*

My sister Linda works for a software company. Her work is top secret. She ¹ *has to* be very careful about security. She ² _____ talk about her work outside the company. If you visit her at work, you ³ _____ go into her office. You ⁴ _____ wait outside. Linda likes the job because she has flexible hours. She ⁵ _____ be at work at a certain time. But sometimes she ⁶ _____ work very long hours.

c What do you have to do for your job or for school?

3 Vocabulary: Jobs and responsibilities

a **AUDIO** Listen. Look at the pictures and repeat the words. Mark the main stress.

1 an accountant   3 a musician   5 a receptionist   7 a lawyer

2 an engineer   4 a mechanic   6 a journalist   8 a taxi driver

b Work with a partner. Talk about the jobs. Use *have to.*

Example   *A taxi driver doesn't have to wear a suit. A lawyer usually has to wear a suit.*

wear a suit			
have a university degree	work at night	go to meetings	use special equipment
	travel a lot	work with people	take notes

4 ▶ Reading

a Describe the situation in the picture.

b Read the article. What is telecommuting?

TELECOMMUTING

"When I arrived in Johannesburg, I jumped into a rental car and drove to a game reserve. But I had a report to send to London, so I parked next to an elephant eating a small tree and e-mailed London."

Christopher Davis is a virtual attorney, one of a growing number of telecommuters working from home or other locations far away from their offices. He stays in contact with clients and co-workers worldwide through e-mail, his cell phone, and the Internet.

It's not just well-paid attorneys who can work wherever they like. Sales people or computer technicians, for example, can often work from home, at least part-time, using their home computers. Anna Brady lives in Dublin, Ireland, and works for a company with offices in California and New York. "Only one or two people in the company work at the main office," she says. "It's often a surprise to meet your colleagues in real life."

Telecommuting is becoming more and more popular. Many employers like it because they save space, energy, and heating costs. Some employees like it because they can choose their own hours. Others would just rather work alone than look at the person at the next desk.

c Read the article again. Write T (true) or F (false).

1	Christopher Davis is a telecommuter.	_T_
2	Telecommuters work in an office at a company.	___
3	Telecommuters use computers and telephones a lot.	___
4	A salesperson can't be a telecommuter.	___
5	Some telecommuters live far from the company they work for.	___
6	Some people don't like to work in an office with other people.	___

d Match a word on the left with a definition on the right.

1	an attorney	_1d_	a	not full-time
2	a client	___	b	a person who works for a company
3	a cell phone	___	c	making a lot of money
4	part-time	___	d	a lawyer
5	an employee	___	e	a person who pays a professional for a service
6	well-paid	___	f	travel to and from work
7	commute	___	g	a mobile telephone

e Work with a partner. How many advantages to telecommuting can you think of? Can you think of any disadvantages?

5 ▶ Focus on Grammar

a Read the last sentence of the article on page 61 (Others would just rather…).

What does this sentence mean?
a Some people don't like to work alone.   b Some people would prefer to work alone.

Would rather, would prefer to		
I / You He / She We / They	**would rather work** **would rather not work** **would prefer to work** **would prefer not to work**	alone.
Questions		
Would you rather work **Would you prefer to work**	alone or with other people?	

Note: *Would* is usually contracted in speaking. *I'd prefer to /I'd rather work alone.*

b Complete the conversations. Use *would rather, would prefer, would you rather,* or *would you prefer.*

1 A: _____ work at night or during the day?
   B: Most people _____ to work during the day, but I _____ work at night. It's quieter.
2 A: _____ to work in the accounts department or _____ stay in sales?
   B: I _____ stay in sales because the pay is better.

c Work with a partner. Discuss the choices. Use *would rather* and *would prefer.*

Example   A: *Would you rather work alone or with other people?*
          B: *I'd rather work with other people.*

work alone or with other people   **have flexible hours or the same schedule every day**
work in a large company or in a small one   **have a boss or be a boss**
travel a lot or stay close to home

6 ▶ Writing

a Read the message to an online forum. What reasons does Seth give for his opinion?

b Write a message to the forum about telecommuting. Give two or three reasons to support your opinion.

c Work with a partner. Exchange papers. Do you both have the same opinion?

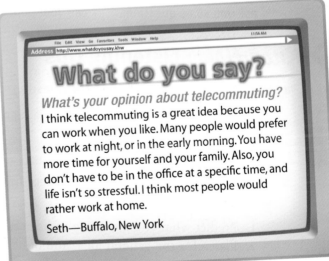

File Edit View Go Favorites Tools Window Help   11:58 AM
Address http://www.whatdoyousay.khw

What do you say?

What's your opinion about telecommuting?
I think telecommuting is a great idea because you can work when you like. Many people would prefer to work at night, or in the early morning. You have more time for yourself and your family. Also, you don't have to be in the office at a specific time, and life isn't so stressful. I think most people would rather work at home.

Seth—Buffalo, New York

Language in Action: Permission

a **AUDIO** What three things does Frank want to do? Listen. Then read.

Frank: Can I put my stuff over here?

Cora: Oh yes, of course. Put it wherever you like.

Frank: Thank you. Do you mind if I open the window? It's a bit warm.

Cora: No, not at all. Go ahead.

Frank: Thanks. Oh, and…is it OK to smoke?

Cora: I'm sorry. You can't smoke in the building. You have to go outside.

Frank: Oh, OK.

b Complete the phrases in the chart with examples from the conversation.

ASKING FOR PERMISSION	SAYING YES	SAYING NO
Can I _____? Is it OK to _____?	Yes, of _____. Go _____.	I'm sorry. You can't _____. (Give a reason.)
Do you mind if I _____?	No, _____ I don't mind.	Please don't.

c Practice with a partner. Use the expressions below.

Example   A: *Is it OK to open the door?*
          B: *Go ahead.*

open the door / window   sit here   call you tomorrow
ask you some questions   use your pen   borrow some money

KnowHow: Listening tips

a Work with a partner. Discuss the questions.

1 List three ways that listening to a recording is different from listening to a person face-to-face.
2 Which do you think is easier?

b Review these ideas for listening to recordings in class. Which ones can you also use in face-to-face listening? Explain.

1 Predict what you are going to hear.
2 Listen for the general idea. You don't have to understand every word.
3 Use key words to help you understand.
4 Listen more than once.

9 ▶ Listening

a Look at the pictures.

   1   Identify the following:

   a guide dog   a trainer   a blindfold

   2   What do you think? What do guide dog trainers do?

b AUDIO Listen to the conversation with a guide dog trainer. What does she like about her job?

c AUDIO Listen again. Fill in the blanks with the expressions below.

   every day   ten days   one month   six months   three years

   1   The guide dog training program lasts _three years_.
   2   All trainers have to wear a blindfold for _____.
   3   Emily works with the dogs _____.
   4   It takes _____ to train a dog.
   5   Trainers work with dogs and owners together for _____.

d What do you think is the most difficult thing about Emily's job?

10 ▶ Speaking

a Put these jobs in order of preference, 1–5. (1 = the job you would like best)

an ice cream vendor   **a window dresser**   **a street performer**   **a zoo keeper**   **a driving instructor**

___   ___   ___   ___   ___

b Work with a partner. Compare your answers. Explain the order you chose.

c What is your ideal job? Why is it your ideal job?

11 Personal style

✔ Clothing and appearances
✔ Modifiers; possessive forms

1 ▶ Vocabulary: Clothes

a Work with a partner. Look at the photographs. Write the letter(s) of the person or people wearing each item or *N* for no one.

Item	Person / people
1 a hat	
2 a T-shirt	
3 a skirt and a blouse	
4 a suit	
5 jeans	
6 a shirt and a tie	
7 a dress	
8 a coat	
9 pants and a jacket	
10 sneakers	
11 shorts	
12 a scarf	

b **AUDIO** Listen to the sentences. Identify the person. Then repeat each sentence.

Example
You hear: *He's wearing shorts and an orange T-shirt.*
You write: *F*

1 __   2 __   3 __   4 __

c What clothing styles are popular where you live?

2 ▶ Listening

a Richard Arroyo is a successful attorney. Look at the picture. Which of these words would you use to describe his clothes? Use a dictionary if necessary.

   casual   formal   conservative   fashionable

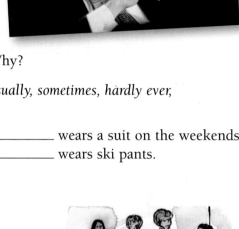

b [AUDIO] Listen to the interview and answer the questions.

   1 What kind of clothes does Richard wear during the week? Why?
   2 What kind of clothes does he wear on weekends? Why?

c [AUDIO] Listen again. Fill in the blanks with these words: *usually, sometimes, hardly ever,* or *never.*

   1 Richard _____ wears a tie.   3 He _____ wears a suit on the weekends.
   2 He _____ wears casual clothes to work.   4 He _____ wears ski pants.

d Do you think clothes affect your opinion of people?

3 ▶ Focus on Grammar

a The woman in the picture is deciding what to buy for a business trip. Which outfit is…

   1 too formal? __   2 too casual? __   3 formal enough? __

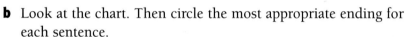

b Look at the chart. Then circle the most appropriate ending for each sentence.

   1 I need a warmer jacket. This one is (not warm enough / really warm / pretty warm).
   2 I love these shoes. They're (too comfortable / very comfortable / not very comfortable).
   3 You can't wear that old T-shirt to work. It's (too casual / pretty casual / not casual enough).

Modifiers		
This tie is (not)	**too**	conservative.
My style is (not)	**very**	comfortable.
On weekends, I'm	**really**	casual.
My jacket is	**pretty**	warm.
These pants are (not)	big	**enough.**

c Work with a partner. Make sentences using the ideas below.

   Example   *A T-shirt is too casual for a wedding.*

A dark suit	is	too	warm		for a job interview.
Jeans	isn't	very	uncomfortable		for a wedding.
A T-shirt	are	really	practical	(enough)	for a hike.
Sneakers	aren't	pretty	casual		for a skiing trip.
A winter jacket			formal		

4 ▶ Language in Action: Advice and suggestions

AUDIO Listen. Complete the conversation. Use the phrases in the chart.

Alex: ¹ _What do you think of_ this jacket?

Eva: It's very nice, but I don't think it's big enough.

Alex: Hmm. Yes.

Eva: ² _____ look for a larger one.

Alex: That's a good idea…
And ³_____ pants _____ buy?

Eva: ⁴_____ buy those? They look good.

Alex: They're not too long?

Eva: I don't think so.

ASKING FOR ADVICE	MAKING SUGGESTIONS
Which… should I…?	Why don't you…?
What do you think of…?	Maybe you should….

5 ▶ *KnowHow*: Intonation in questions

a **AUDIO** Listen to the intonation in *wh-* and *yes / no* questions. Which type of question goes up at the end? Which type does not?

Wh- questions	*Yes / No questions*
1 Which pants should I wear?	Should I wear the blue ones?
2 What do you think of this jacket?	Do you like it?
3 Why don't you wear your leather jacket?	Do you mean this one?

b **AUDIO** Listen again and repeat the questions.

c Practice the conversation in section 4 with appropriate intonation.

6 ▶ Speaking

Work with a partner. Make conversations for one or both of these situations.

7 In Conversation

AUDIO Whose briefcase is it? Listen. Then read.

Waiter: Excuse me. Is this your briefcase?
Anne: No. It's not mine. Is it yours, Melanie?
Melanie: No. Mine is right here. I think it's his.
Waiter: Whose?
Melanie: The tall guy with the beard. He's just leaving now.
Waiter: Thanks. Sir! Excuse me…

8 Focus on Grammar

a Look at the chart and circle the correct answer.

Use possessive pronouns (before / in place of) a noun.

Possessive forms

Whose briefcase is this? (Whose is this?)

Possessive adjective + noun	Possessive pronoun
It's **my** briefcase.	It's **mine**.
They're **your** notes.	They're **yours**.
That's **his** sweater.	That's **his**.
It's **her** jacket.	It's **hers**.
Is that **our** car?	No, the other one is **ours**.
That's **their** house.	It's **theirs**.

▼ **Help Desk**

Don't confuse *they're* and *their!*

their = possessive adjective:
*That's **their** house.*

they're = they are:
***They're** (the pants are) too long.*

b Circle the correct answers.

1 A: I think that's (your / yours) sweater over there.
  B: No, it's not. It's Jay's. (My / Mine) is red.
2 A: Is Jane's car the same as (our / ours)?
  B: Well, (her / hers) is the same kind, but (our / ours) car is older.

c Look at the illustration. Then match the sentences and the pictures.

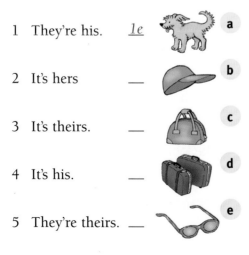

1 They're his.   *1e*   **a**

2 It's hers   —   **b**

3 It's theirs.   —   **c**

4 It's his.   —   **d**

5 They're theirs. —   **e**

68

9 Vocabulary: Appearance

Look at the chart. Then fill in the blanks. Use *she's, she has, he's,* or *he has.*

He / She is	in his / her 20s middle-aged	tall short	overweight thin
He / She has	blonde hair a mustache	straight hair blue eyes	dark / light skin glasses

1   _She's_ young.
2   _____ middle-aged.
3   _____ probably in her twenties.
4   _____ pretty tall and slim.
5   _____ short and a little overweight.
6   _____ light hair and a mustache.
7   _____ short, curly hair, and glasses.

10 Writing

a   Read the descriptions. Underline the words and expressions that help you to imagine the person's appearance.

b   Look again at the people on page 65. Choose one to describe. Name the person. Make notes about his or her appearance.

c   Use your notes to write a description of the person. Write five sentences.

d   Read other students' descriptions. Who are they describing?

▼ Help Desk

What does he look like? =
Give a physical description of him.

He looks like a rock star. =
He is similar to a rock star in appearance.

My mother-in-law is nearly ninety years old, but she's still in good health and very independent. She's very short, with thin, white hair, and she wears glasses. She usually wears a black or blue dress, or a skirt and a blouse, and she always wears some jewelry...

My friend Sam is tall and fairly thin. He has dark skin, long dark hair, a beard, and brown eyes. People say he looks like a rock star. He usually wears jeans and a sweater, and he likes to wear a scarf. He never wears

11 ▷ Reading

a Look at the pictures. What do you think this story is about?

b Read the story. Who did John Blanchard speak to in the train station?

The Rose

John Blanchard studied the people in the station. He was looking for a girl whose heart he loved, but whose face he had never seen.

Blanchard first became interested in Hollis Maynell when he found a book in a Florida library. The handwritten notes on the pages fascinated him. They showed a thoughtful personality and a sharp mind. A name was written in the front of the book: Miss Hollis Maynell. She lived in New York City.

Blanchard wrote to Hollis Maynell for over a year, and slowly a friendship developed into something more. Blanchard asked for a photograph, but Maynell refused. She felt that if he really cared, it would not matter what she looked like. Finally she agreed to a meeting: 7:00 p.m. at Grand Central Station in New York. "You'll recognize me," she wrote, "by the rose I'll wear on my coat." Now Blanchard was there, waiting for the woman he knew he loved.

Suddenly Blanchard saw a young woman coming through the crowd. Her figure was tall and slim. Her blonde hair lay back in curls from her delicate ears; her eyes were as blue as flowers. In her pale green suit she was like the springtime come alive. Blanchard moved towards her automatically. He didn't notice that she was not wearing a rose.

Then he saw Hollis Maynell. She was standing behind the girl. A woman past 40, she had gray hair and a pale, round face under an old hat. Her gray eyes had a warm and kind look.

Blanchard hesitated for a moment. Then he hid his disappointment and spoke to the older woman. "I'm John Blanchard, and you must be Miss Maynell. I am so glad you could meet me. May I take you to dinner?"

The older woman smiled. "I don't know what this is about, son," she answered, "but that young lady in the green coat asked me to wear this rose. And she said that if you asked me out to dinner, I should tell you that she is waiting for you in the restaurant across the street."

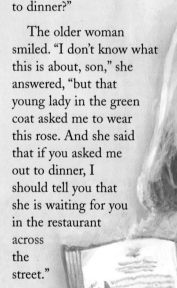

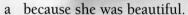

c Match beginnings and endings.

1 Blanchard wrote to Hollis Maynell   _1b_
2 He didn't know what Hollis Maynell looked like   __
3 He noticed the young woman first   __
4 He spoke to the older woman   __
5 Hollis Maynell didn't wear a rose   __

a because she was beautiful.
b because he read her notes in a book.
c because she was wearing a rose.
d because she didn't give him a photograph.
e because she wanted to test Blanchard's love.

d Work with a partner. Discuss the questions.

1 What do you think of this story?
2 How do you think the story might continue?
3 What do you think the main idea of the story is?

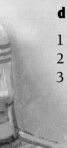

12 Plans and ambitions

✔ Education and careers
✔ *To* and *because*; *would like to, want to, plan to, be going to*

1 ▶ In Conversation

a **AUDIO** What reasons does each person give for studying English? Listen. Then read.

Why Are You Studying English?

I'm going to English classes to improve my speaking and listening. If I speak English well, I can get a better job.

–Ulla Schmidt
Bern, Switzerland

I want to go to a university and get a degree in business. I need English for a career in international business.

–Joseph Kitonga
Merca, Somalia

I don't have a choice! I have to take an exam in English every year. If I don't pass, I have to take extra classes.

–Alan Lin
Beijing, China

I'm studying English because I'm going to be a pilot. English classes are part of our training program.

–Ricardo Flores
Cartago, Costa Rica

I love to visit the United States. My sister lives there, and I often visit her. I take classes to keep up my level of English.

–Lídia Pereira
Belo Horizonte, Brazil

b Whose reasons are similar to yours?

2 ▶ Vocabulary: School and careers

a Answer the questions about the words in **bold**. If necessary, look at the interviews again.

1 Where do you go to get a **degree**?
2 What is the difference between a **class** and a **training program**?
3 What is a **career**? What is a **job**?
4 What is the difference between **taking** an exam and **passing** an exam?

b Look back at the interviews. Write the verbs that are used before each noun below.

an exam	a university	classes	a better job
take an exam			

c Work with a partner. Discuss what someone has to do in your country to become:

a doctor   a flight attendant   a university professor   a bank clerk

3 ▶ Focus on Grammar

a Look at the chart. Then underline sentences that express reasons with *to* and *because* in the interviews on page 71.

To and *because* for purpose and reasons	
to + verb	
I'm studying English	**to practice** conversation. **to get** a better job.
because + subject + verb	
I'm studying English	**because I like** it. **because it's** an international language.

b Match the beginnings and endings.

1	Dolores is studying medicine	_1c_	a	because I have an exam tomorrow.
2	I have to study tonight	__	b	to become flight attendants.
3	They have to take the exam again	__	c	because she wants to be a doctor.
4	They're taking a training program	__	d	because they didn't pass it the first time.
5	My cousin Ann moved to Atlanta	__	e	to finish his degree in music.
6	Tom is going to a college in Boston	__	f	to be with her mother.

c Work with a partner. Think of two reasons why people do each of the following:

take classes   buy computers   leave jobs   move away from home

Examples *People take classes to learn new skills.*
People take classes because they want better jobs.

4 ▶ Speaking

a Look at the list of classes at a local college. Choose two classes that you would like to take. Use the list or your own ideas.

b Work with a partner. Say which classes you chose and why.

Example *I chose "Taking Better Photographs," because I'm interested in photography, but I can't take good photos.*

COURSES

Summer

▶ The Internet and International Business
▶ Introduction to Computer Programming
▶ Introduction to Web Design
▶ Acting for Beginners
▶ The History of Rock Music
▶ Taking Better Photographs
▶ Beginning Japanese
▶ Peruvian Art and Architecture

5 ▶ Reading

a Work with a partner. Discuss these questions.

1 Does your education end when you finish school?
2 Why do working adults sometimes go back to school?

b Read the article. Find two reasons why many people take continuing education classes.

Students For Life: Workers Need Continuing Education

Every Tuesday evening, Sonya Farrar leaves her job as a legal assistant and drives to a local college to take classes in Business Law. Although Sonya already has a degree and several years of experience, she wants to learn more. The classes help her to stay ahead in her job. Eventually, Sonya would like to get a higher-paying position in the company where she works.

Sonya's husband, Gustavo, also takes night classes. After ten years as a computer programmer, Gustavo lost his job last year. He was always interested in teaching, so he decided to get a degree in education. Now he hopes to teach high school computer classes.

Sonya and Gustavo are typical of many working Americans who are returning to the classroom to continue their education. The numbers are growing fast. In 1999, 46 percent of American adults, almost half of the adult population, were enrolled in an adult education program. Just nine years earlier, the number was 32 percent.

Why is this happening? Many adults, like Sonya, feel that they need continuing education just to keep up with the changes in their field. People who studied business fifteen years ago probably did not take classes in information systems, for example. Now they need to go back to school.

Other workers, like Gustavo, go back to school to train for a new career. Gustavo now feels that losing his job was not all bad. "I was very upset at first," he admits. "But now I'm glad that I'm going back to school. I want to do something different."

c Underline the following words in the text. Then write one of the words next to each of the definitions. (1) = paragraph number.

a legal assistant (1)   enrolled (3)   keep up with (4)
eventually (1)   field (4)   train (5)

1 a person who works for a lawyer or a group of lawyers: _a legal assistant_
2 to learn a specific skill: _____
3 after some time, in the end: _____
4 an area of study or work: _____
5 registered in an educational program: _____
6 to know what is happening, to stay up to date: _____

d What kind of continuing education is popular where you live?

6 Focus on Grammar

a Look at the chart. Which two sentences are about wishes? Which two are about plans?

Would like to, want to, plan to, be going to			
Affirmative		**Negative**	
I'd like to I want to I plan to I'm (You're, He's...) **going to**	do something different.	I wouldn't like to I don't want to I don't plan to I'm not going to	change careers.

b Fill in the blanks with the correct forms of the verbs in parentheses.

1 My friend Nicole _would like to_ (like) be a police officer. She _____ (go) take a test next month.

2 We _____ (go) get married next month but we _____ (not plan) have children.

3 Jack _____ (want) learn Chinese because he _____ (like) go to China some day.

4 Patricia _____ (not go) take a job in Florida because she _____ (not want) move.

c Work with a partner. **A**, you won $50,000. **B**, ask questions about A's plans.

Example   B: *What are you going to do with the money?*
A: *I'm going to…*

7 Language in Action: Probability

a [AUDIO] Listen to the actor answering questions about his plans. Which of his plans is the most certain? Which one is the least certain?

take time off   **start a family**   **live in Hollywood**

b [AUDIO] Listen again. Check the expressions that you hear.

	EXPRESSING PROBABILITY		
NO	__ Definitely not.	__ No way.	
↓	__ Probably not.	__ I don't think so.	
	__ I don't know.	__ I'm not sure.	__ Maybe.
	__ Probably.	__ I think so.	
YES	__ Definitely.	__ Of course.	

c Work with a partner. Ask and answer questions about your plans in three of these areas. Use the expressions above.

work   home   school   entertainment   travel

> ▼ **Help Desk**
>
> Sometimes in informal speech *going to* sounds like *gonna*, *want to* sounds like *wanna*, and *don't know* sounds like *dunno*.

8 ▶ Writing

a Read the letter. What plans does Sandra describe in paragraphs 1 and 2? How do you think these paragraphs continue?

124 Winding Way
Portland

April 23

Dear Linda,

Thank you for your letter. It was so nice to hear from you. I'm glad that you and your family are well. I'm still working at the bank, but I want to get a better job. I'm going to take classes in computer programming in the fall because I want to learn more computer skills. I'd really like to get a job near my home because

I'm still looking forward to the summer. I'm going to take two weeks off, and we plan to travel to the north to visit some friends of mine in

Anyway, that's all my news for now. Write back soon!
Best wishes,
Sandra

b Underline some useful phrases above for beginning and ending a letter.

c You are going to write a letter to a friend about your plans for the near future. Think of two types of plans you would like to write about. Make some notes.

d Write your letter. Try to write one page.

e Read your letter again. Correct all the mistakes you find.

9 ▶ *KnowHow*: Writing tips

a Here are some suggestions for writing a letter or a short composition in English. Match each suggestion to one of the stages (b–e) in section 8.

___ Think about what you want to write. Make some notes.
___ When you start writing, concentrate on what you want to say. Don't stop to think too much about grammar or vocabulary.
___ Use a model for useful phrases and layout.
___ Wait a while. Then read your letter again and make corrections.

b Which of these strategies do you find the most useful?

10 ▶ Listening

a Look at the headline. What did this man do, and why?

Burned Out At 25

• • • • • • • • • • • • • • • •

Investment banker Barry Miller gives up $150,000 job to follow his dreams.

b **AUDIO** Listen to the conversation and answer the questions.

1 Why did Barry give up his job?
2 What are his plans now?

c **AUDIO** Listen again. Circle the correct answer.

1 Barry started work when he was ___.
  a 20   b 25   c 30
2 He worked ___ hours a week.
  a 40   b 50   c 100
3 Which of these is true?
  a Barry has children.   b Barry doesn't have children. c He doesn't say.
4 In his last job, Barry ___.
  a wanted to make money b didn't make money   c didn't want to make money
5 Barry does not want to ___.
  a travel   b go back to his job   c study drama

d What do you think of Barry's decision?

11 ▶ Speaking

a What are your priorities for the future? Look at the list below. Put the items in order of importance to you. (1 = most important)

  ___ a job that you enjoy   ___ a good education   ___ friends
  ___ a husband or wife   ___ a lot of money   ___ travel
  ___ good health   ___ family   ___ (other): _____

b Work in groups. Compare your lists. Give reasons for your answers.

Grammar

1 Read the text. How do Andy and Madee feel about their city? What do they want to do?

WORKING FOR A DREAM
Andy Liu and Madee Chuan-Liu are young people with a plan. They both work in one of the most successful clothing companies in Bangkok, but they would really like to open a small hotel in the country. "We meet a lot of interesting people in the city," Madee says. "But it's noisy, and we'd like a quieter life." Andy says, "If you want to live your dream, you have to plan ahead." They are saving money, and they are going to leave the city in a couple of years to make their dream a reality.

2 Complete the letter with *to*, *because*, or *N*. (*N*=nothing)

Dear Kelly,
I hope you're fine. Things are pretty good here. We are working hard ¹_____ save money, but there are times when I'd rather not ²_____ do this job. I'd prefer ³_____ work part-time, but there is too much I have ⁴_____ do every day. We plan ⁵_____ take a trip to the country soon ⁶_____ we want ⁷_____ find a good place for our hotel. I'd love ⁸_____ talk to you about our plans. Could I ⁹_____ call you at work sometime? It's hard to call at a normal time ¹⁰_____ I have a busy schedule!
      Your friend,
      Madee

3 Circle the correct sentences.

1. a It's the most expensive hotel.
   b It's the hotel most expensive.
2. a Our work is not enough exciting.
   b Our work is not exciting enough.
3. a We would rather live in the country.
   b We rather would live in the country.
4. a I plan to buy an office here.
   b I plan buy an office here.

4 Madee and Andy are getting ready for their trip to the country. Complete the conversation using adjectives and *too* or (*not*) *enough*.

Madee: We don't need to take formal clothes. These clothes are ¹ *too formal*_____.

Andy: You're right. And we have to find a cheaper car. That rental car is ²_____.

Madee: OK, I'll call some other places. Do we have a bigger suitcase? This one isn't ³_____.

Andy: I think there's one in the closet.

Madee: What did you say? This apartment is ⁴_____! It will be nice to be in a quieter place!

5 Correct the mistakes in the sentences.

1. I can find your passport, but I can't find my.
2. Andy's father is lawyer in a big firm.
3. This is the more boring job in the world!
4. She doesn't has to work so many hours.
5. Donna is optimistic more than Susan.
6. They would prefer open their hotel now.
7. They are saving money because to start their own business.
8. Is this yours wallet?

Vocabulary

6 ▶ Circle the correct answers.

1 He studied for four years at a university
  and then ___ a good job.
  a passed   b visited   c got

2 Being a pilot is a ___ job because so many
  things can go wrong.
  a boring   b comfortable   c stressful

3 He got a ___ in English from Brown
  University and now works as a teacher.
  a degree   b course   c career

4 A ___ is a person who writes for
  newspapers and magazines.
  a chef   b journalist   c lawyer

5 The same ___ designed three of the bridges
  in our city.
  a musician b mechanic   c engineer

7 ▶ What do Madee and Andy look like?
Describe them.

Example
*Madee is pretty
short. She is
very slim.
She has…*

Fun Spot

Use the letters from this word to make words
that fit the clues below.

THEATERS

Example You do this with food = <u>E</u> <u>A</u> <u>T</u>

People wear these on their heads =
__ __ __ __

Another word for "begin" = __ __ __ __ __

Recycling Center

8 ▶ Complete the paragraph with the correct past
tense forms of the verbs.

Andy ¹____ (come) to Bangkok from Buffalo, New
York in 1999. He only ²____ (have) $1000 and
some clothes and books. He ³____ (find) a place to
live and started to look for a job right away. He
⁴____ (give) his application to every design
company in the city, but nobody called him so he
⁵____ (take) a job in a restaurant. He ⁶____ (make)
very little money there, and he wasn't very happy.
Then the manager of Maya Fashions called him,
so Andy ⁷____ (buy) a new suit and ⁸____ (go) for
an interview. The manager liked him a lot, so
Andy ⁹____ (get) the job, and that evening he
¹⁰____ (write) to his friends in Buffalo to tell them
about his good luck.

9 ▶ Write the questions for the answers.

1 *Are you working on your project?*
  (your project)
  Yes, I'm working on it now.

2 _____?
  (When)
  They arrived at the concert at 8 o'clock.

3 _____?
  (How / cookies)
  There are two cookies in the jar.

4 _____?
  (How / coffee)
  I drink three cups.

5 _____?
  (Madee / to the party)
  No, she didn't. She stayed home last
  night.

6 _____?
  (fireworks)
  Yes, we did. We saw them clearly.

Where you drive a car = __ __ __ __ __ __

Continue the game. How many more words can
you find?

✔ Friendship and love
✔ Words ending in *-one, -thing, -where;* subject / object questions

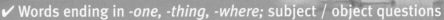

❘ Reading

a Work with a partner. Discuss the questions.

1 Where do you go if you want to meet new friends?
2 Look at the newspaper headline. What do you think it means?

b Read the article. How is Singles Night at the supermarket different from other nights?

Singles Find a New Place to Meet:

at the SUPERMARKET

On a recent Thursday night, Clara Allen went to her local supermarket to look for something different. Not dish detergent or a pound of vegetables, but a nice man. She was not the only one. Dozens of singles attended "Singles Night" at the Fresh Fields Whole Foods market near Washington, D.C. The store started the monthly event in June, and the evenings have become very popular.

Meeting by the organic vegetables may sound unromantic, but for many people it is a good alternative to night clubs. "I like this better," said Clara Allen, 34, a recreation specialist dressed in jeans and a white blouse. "No one is drinking. No one is smoking. And you don't have to shout."

For a five-dollar contribution, singles write their names on a white button and use stickers to announce their hobbies. They can also listen to live music and watch modern dance and even ballet in the grocery store. Not everyone could relax. One local

> People meet new friends in many different ways.

businessman, uncomfortable in a gray suit, put his button in his pocket. "I'm shy," he admitted.

Clara Allen's evening was a success. She met Rob, a 44-year-old marketing manager, while buying some cake in the baked goods department. The two discussed their lives and their jobs, and found out they had a lot in common.

c Read the article again. Circle the correct answer.

1 Singles Night is held ___.
   a every month   b every June   c every Thursday
2 Clara Allen likes Singles Night at the supermarket because ___.
   a it's like a night club   b it's quiet   c people are drinking
3 The businessman was uncomfortable because he ___.
   a didn't like the music   b didn't have a   c was nervous meeting
                              button   new people
4 Clara's evening was a success because she ___.
   a bought some cake   b met someone new   c listened to live music

d What do you think? Is Singles Night at the supermarket a good idea? Why (not)?

2 Focus on Grammar

▼ **Help Desk**

Words with *every* are singular.

Everybody **is** mad at me.

Everything **looks** good.

a Look at the chart and answer the questions.

1 What words are used with a negative verb?
   a words with *some*   b words with *any*   c words with *no*

2 Which two sentences in each column have the same meaning?

Words ending in *-one*, *-thing*, *-where*		
A person: -one*	**A thing: -thing**	**A place: -where**
I met **everyone**.	I saw **everything**.	I went **everywhere**.
I met **someone**.	I saw **something**.	I went **somewhere**.
I met **no one**.	I saw **nothing**.	I went **nowhere**.
I did**n't** meet **anyone**.	I did**n't** see **anything**.	I did**n't** go **anywhere**.

***Note:** You can also use *-body*.   *everybody, somebody, nobody, anybody*

b Imagine that there were 50 people at the Singles Night at the supermarket. Circle the number of people the underlined word refers to.

1 Everyone wore a white button.   0   1   50
2 The businessman didn't meet anyone.   0   1   50
3 Clara met someone in the baked goods department.   0   1   50
4 No one smoked or drank.   0   1   50

c Complete the conversations with the words below.

anything   anybody   no one   everyone   something   anywhere   nothing

1 A: You went somewhere last night.   B: No! I didn't go *anywhere.*
2 A: There's something wrong.   B: No, there is _____ wrong. I'm OK.
3 A: You met someone.   B: No! I didn't meet _____!
4 A: Everybody's mad at me.   B: Don't be silly! _____'s mad at you.
5 A: She told you everything.   B: You're wrong. She didn't tell me _____.
6 A: Were there a lot of people at the party? B: Yes! _____ was there.
7 A: Do you want to speak to me?   B: Yes. I'd like to ask you _____.

3 ▸ Vocabulary: Relationships

a Work with a partner. Match the expressions with the definitions.

1 get together (with friends):   *1e*   a to invite someone to do something
2 get along (with someone):   ___   b to be in a romantic relationship
3 go out (with someone):   ___   c to end a romantic relationship
4 ask someone out (on a date):   ___   d to like someone, have a good relationship
5 break up (with someone):   ___   e to spend time with

b Fill in the blanks with the correct form of one of the expressions (1–5) above.

1 Tim is Sally's boyfriend. She's _going out_ with him.
2 My boss and I don't agree on anything. I don't _____ _____ with her at all.
3 Cindy and Stan aren't going to get married. They _____ _____ last month.
4 If you like Barbara, you should _____ her _____.
5 Let's _____ _____ soon. Would you like to come to our house for dinner?

4 ▸ Language in Action: Favors

a **AUDIO** What's the problem? Listen. Then read.

Joe: Hey, Patrick, could you do me a favor?
Patrick: Sure. What do you need?
Joe: Would you mind giving me a ride home later? My car's in the shop.
Patrick: Not at all.
Joe: Thanks. I'd appreciate it.

b Complete the phrases in the chart with examples from the conversation.

ASKING A FAVOR	SAYING YES	THANKING
Could you _____ a favor?	Of course. _____	Thank you (very much). Thanks (a lot.) I'd _____ it.
Would you mind _____?	Not at all.	

c Practice the conversation above with a partner. Use your own names and ideas. Here are some suggestions.

help me clean up   **lend me some money**   **go to the supermarket**

> ▼ **Help Desk**
>
> Don't forget to use verb + *-ing* after *Would you mind...*
>
> *Would you mind **helping** me?*

5 Listening

a Look at the picture. Carol is talking to her friend Laura. What do you think they are talking about?

b [AUDIO] Listen to the conversation. What does Laura tell Carol about Patrick?

c Answer the questions with *Patrick*, *Joe*, or *Amanda*.

1 Who did Carol meet?	*Patrick*
2 Who introduced her to Patrick?	_____
3 Who works with Patrick?	_____
4 Who invited Patrick?	_____
5 Who went out with Patrick?	_____
6 Who asked Carol out?	_____

6 Focus on Grammar

a Look at the chart. Circle the correct answers below.

1 Subject questions (use / don't use) *do*, *does*, or *did*.
2 Object questions (use / don't use) *do*, *does*, or *did*.

Subject / object questions				
Subject questions			***Object questions***	
Carol likes Patrick.			Carol likes Patrick	
Who likes Patrick?	Carol.		**Who does** Carol **like?**	Patrick.
Joe introduced Patrick.			Joe introduced Patrick.	
Who introduced Patrick?	Joe.		**Who did** Joe **introduce?**	Patrick.

b Write questions for the underlined words.

1 *Where did you go?*   I went to a party <u>somewhere</u> last night.
2 _____ <u>Someone</u> invited me.
3 _____ I met <u>someone</u>.
4 _____ We talked about <u>something</u>.
5 _____ We ate <u>something</u>.
6 _____ <u>Someone</u> drove me home.

c Work with a partner. Make a conversation with the questions above. Use your imagination to answer the questions. Then change roles.

Example   A: *Where did you go last night?* —B: *To the tennis club.*
                A: *Who invited you?* —B: *Cassandra.*

d Work with a partner. Discuss the questions.

1 Who do you call most often? Who calls you?
2 Who sometimes asks you for favors? Who do you ask?
3 Who did you meet recently? Who introduced you?

7 Vocabulary: Personality characteristics

a Read the interviews. Why do these people like their friends?

Who's Your Best Friend?

Nicole Brouwer, Amsterdam, Holland

My best friend's name is Shelly. We call each other at least once a week. She and I are opposites in every way. I'm pretty shy, but she's outgoing and has a lot of friends. And she's very outspoken. She says exactly what she thinks. I don't like to upset people.

Dante Young, Arima, Trinidad and Tobago

I guess I'm unusual because my grandfather is my best friend. I tell him everything. He's just so optimistic about life. He always sees the bright side of things. And he makes me laugh. He's a lot of fun to be with because he has a great sense of humor.

Lia Hamada, Detroit, Michigan

My best friend is a guy. His name's Jamie. He's also my neighbor. He's just one of the kindest people I know. I always tell him all my problems. If you're in trouble, Jamie will do anything to help you.

b Look at the interviews again. Match the beginnings and endings of the sentences.

1	An **outgoing** person	_1d_	a says what he or she thinks.
2	An **outspoken** person	__	b often makes people laugh.
3	An **optimistic** person	__	c has a positive attitude towards life.
4	A person with a **sense of humor**	__	d is friendly with many people.
5	A **kind** person	__	e helps other people.

Try to match the beginnings and endings of these sentences.

6	An **honest** person	__	f is open to new ideas.
7	A **lazy** person	__	g tells the truth.
8	An **open-minded** person	__	h doesn't like to change his or her plans.
9	A **stubborn** person	__	i does what he or she promises.
10	A **reliable** person	__	j doesn't like to work hard.

c **AUDIO** Listen and check your answers. Repeat the sentences.

d Work with a partner. Choose three words from 7b to describe yourself. Say why you chose each word.

8 ▶ Writing

a Think of a person you know well. Choose three characteristics that describe the person. Give a reason for your choices.

Name:	Helena
Characteristics	**Reasons**
reliable	She always arrives on time.

b Write a paragraph describing the person. In your paragraph, write about…

1 who the person is, how you met, and how often you get together.
2 the three characteristics that best describe the person.

9 ▶ *KnowHow*: Speaking tips

a Read the following paragraph.

My best friend's name is Shelly. We call each other at least once a week. She and I are opposites in every way. I'm pretty shy, but she's outgoing and has a lot of friends.

b **AUDIO** Now read and listen to the same thing spoken spontaneously. How is it different?

" My best friend? Let me see…um…it's Shelly. Yes…she's a good friend. We call each other, I don't know, once a week…no, more than that. She and I are absolutely…we're opposites in every way. Completely different. Like… I'm pretty shy, you know? But she's umm…really outgoing… "

c In the paragraph above, find and underline examples of…

1 correcting a mistake.
2 starting a sentence again.
3 repeating words and ideas.
4 thinking expressions like *let me see*.

d Work with a partner. Talk for thirty seconds about your friends. Use the strategies in 9c.

10 ▶ Speaking

a For each statement below, check the box (1–4) that best describes your opinion.

A good friend…	Agree ⟶ Disagree			
	1	**2**	**3**	**4**
1 is about my age.				
2 is from a similar background (family, education).				
3 has the same interests as I do.				
4 never gets angry with me.				
5 has a similar personality to mine.				
6 is fun to be with.				
7 is easy to talk to.				
8 always tells me the truth.				
9 is someone I have known for a long time.				
10 is hard to find.				

b Work in groups. Compare your answers. Which statements does everybody agree with?

14 Future trends

✔ Computers and new technology
✔ Verbs with two objects; *will / won't, might / might not*

1 ▶ Speaking

a How does technology affect your life? Complete the survey.

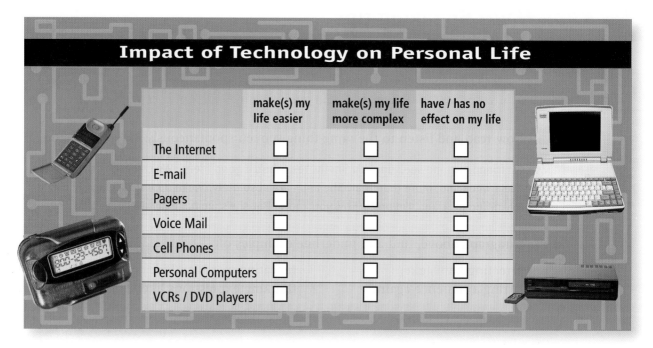

Impact of Technology on Personal Life

	make(s) my life easier	make(s) my life more complex	have / has no effect on my life
The Internet	☐	☐	☐
E-mail	☐	☐	☐
Pagers	☐	☐	☐
Voice Mail	☐	☐	☐
Cell Phones	☐	☐	☐
Personal Computers	☐	☐	☐
VCRs / DVD players	☐	☐	☐

b Work in small groups. Compare your answers. Which items above are the most useful to you?

▼ *Help Desk*

Voice mail is a way of recording spoken telephone messages

2 ▶ In Conversation

AUDIO What does Melissa's phone do? Listen. Then read.

Nadia: Nice phone!
Melissa: Thanks. My dad bought it for me.
Nadia: What do you do with it?
Melissa: Here. Let me show you. You can use it as a phone or to send e-mail. Look. My friend Leo just sent me a message.
Nadia: Oh…I see.
Melissa: But you can also play games on it, or listen to music….
Nadia: Can't you just use a CD player?
Melissa: Yes, but I can't send messages on my CD player.
Nadia: Hmm. I guess not.

3 ▶ Focus on Grammar

a Look at the examples in the chart. Complete these sentences with the words *Nadia* and *the phone*. Notice the order of the words.

Melissa showed _____ to _____.
Melissa showed _____ _____.

Verbs with two objects		
My dad bought	a cell phone me	**for** me. a cell phone.
Leo sent	a message a message Melissa her	**to** Melissa. **to** her. a message. a message.

Note: Some other verbs that take two objects are *give*, *show*, and *tell*. These verbs all use *to*, not *for*.

Object pronouns	
I	me
you	**you**
he	**him**
she	**her**
it	**it**
we	**us**
they	**them**

b Put the words in order to make sentences.

1 bought / their / them / a / parents / car
2 these / Mary / to / glasses / give / please
3 parents / the / my / showed / I / pictures
4 the / she / to / sent / package / us
5 told / grandmother / story / that / me / my
6 that / for / bought / Jeffrey / her / sweater

Their parents bought them a car.
_____
_____
_____
_____
_____

c Say each sentence above in a different way.

Example *Their parents bought a car for them.*

4 ▶ Language in Action: Telephone talk

a **AUDIO** Listen. Melissa is calling Leo. What is Melissa's phone number?

b **AUDIO** Listen again. Number the expressions below in the order that you hear them.

CALLING	TAKING A MESSAGE
___ This is….	*1* Hello?
___ Could you tell him (that) I called?	___ I'm sorry. He's not here right now.
___ Could you give him a message?	___ I'll tell him.
___ Can I speak to…please?	___ Just a minute. Let me write that down.

c Practice phone conversations using your own names and telephone numbers.

5 ▶ Vocabulary: Computers and the Internet

a Find a word in the advertisement that means:

1 connected to the Internet: *online*
2 explore the Internet: _____
3 computer programs: _____
4 take from the Internet: _____

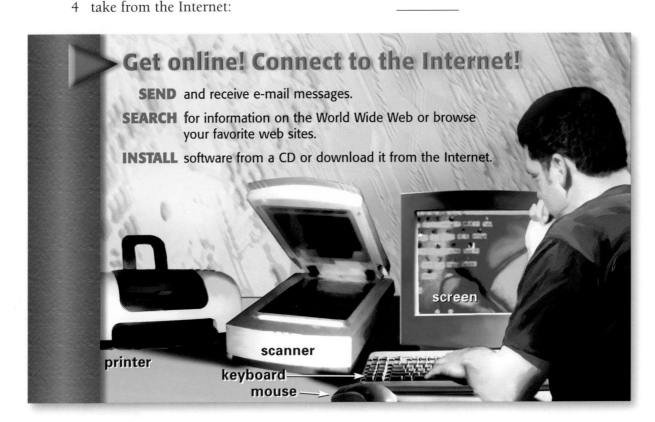

Get online! Connect to the Internet!

SEND and receive e-mail messages.

SEARCH for information on the World Wide Web or browse your favorite web sites.

INSTALL software from a CD or download it from the Internet.

screen

printer   scanner
        keyboard
        mouse

b Work with a partner. Make a list of things that you can do on a computer. Use words from the advertisement above and your own ideas.

Example   *You can listen to CDs on a computer.*

6 ▶ Listening

a Work with a partner. Talk about why people use computers.

b **AUDIO** Listen to Rachel, Noah, and Tony talk about how they use their computers. Who uses the computer at work? Who uses it at home?

c **AUDIO** Listen again. What does each person use a computer for? Check the boxes below.

	E-mail	Entertainment	Travel	Shopping
Rachel				
Noah				
Tony				

7 Focus on Grammar

a Look at these predictions. Which one is less certain than the other? Circle *a* or *b*.

   a Schools might have computer centers instead of libraries.
   b People will always prefer to shop in real stores.

Will, won't, might, might not					
Affirmative			**Negative**		
I / You He / She / It We / They	**will** ('ll) **might**	need computer skills.	I / You He / She / It We / They	**will not** (won't) **might not**	buy a computer.
Questions			**Answers**		
What **will** we need?			Computer skills.		
Will we need computer skills?			Yes, you **will**. You **might**.	No, you **won't**. You **might not**.	

b Complete the predictions below with the verbs given.

1 *might, will:* I am sure that we _____ find intelligent life on other planets—But the first messages _____ take millions of years to get to us.

2 *might, will, won't:* Certainly we _____ see important advances in biology and chemistry. Who knows? We _____ take pills to keep our bodies and minds young. So even people in their 70s _____ look old.

3 *might, might not, will:* People _____ definitely work at home much more, using computers to communicate. So workers _____ have more time for their families. Sometimes people _____ meet their co-workers at all.

c What do you think? Make sentences using the phrases below.

   Example *We might find intelligent life on other planets.*

We Most people Some people	will (probably) (probably) won't might might not	find intelligent life on other planets. take vacations in space. live longer. work less.

8 *KnowHow*: Pronunciation of contractions with *will*

a **AUDIO** Listen. Circle the sentence you hear.

1	I go.	I'll go.	4	They tell you.	They'll tell you.
2	I see.	I'll see.	5	You want it.	You'll want it.
3	We do it.	We'll do it	6	You know.	You'll know.

b **AUDIO** Now listen and repeat. Practice the / l / sound in the contractions.

1	I'll do it.	3	You'll see.	5	We'll call you.	7	She'll know.
2	It'll rain.	4	This'll be difficult.	6	What'll I say?	8	Where'll he go?

9 ▶ Speaking

a Work in groups. Choose two of the categories below. For each category:

1 Look at the pictures. How will these situations be different in the future?
2 Discuss how things will or will not change. Use the ideas given, or your own ideas.

1 TRANSPORTATION
traffic
public transportation

3 COMMUNICATIONS
telephones
e-mail and pagers

2 SHOPPING
cash or credit cards
online shopping

4 ENTERTAINMENT
video, TV, and computer games
home entertainment

b Compare answers with other groups. Do you think life will be better or worse in the future?

10 ▶ Writing

a Read the paragraph about food and cooking in the future. How many changes does the person describe?

> *In the future, I think we will probably cook less, and we will buy more prepared food at the supermarket or online. Who knows? We might use computers in the kitchen, too, to tell us when food in the refrigerator is going bad, or when something is burning on the stove. People like me might not make so many mistakes with cooking!*

b Choose one of the categories in section 9. Write a paragraph about three to five things that will or will not change in that category.

c Work in small groups. Read each other's ideas. Do you agree with them?

Reading

a Look at the pictures and write words that go with the definitions.

1 a sound that warns you of danger: _____
2 the material that clothes are made of: _____
3 the part of a shirt or jacket near the neck: _____
4 something that you wear around your waist: _____

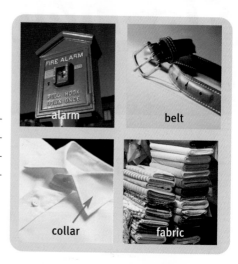

alarm   belt

collar   fabric

b Read the article. What is the main purpose of intelligent clothing? Circle the answer below.

communication   entertainment   temperature   shopping

INTELLIGENT CLOTHING

The phrase "a smart outfit" now has a new meaning. Scientists are developing clothing that in the future may protect us from thieves, identify health problems, and tell us when we forget our keys! This "intelligent clothing" may contain cell phones and mini-computers. T-shirts will know if we're sad or happy and play the appropriate music.

There is already a T-shirt on the market that measures heart rate and temperature. Sensors in the fabric send the data through a type of pager attached to a belt. Older people and people with illnesses can use the clothing to send an alarm to the nearest hospital.

Another example of intelligent clothing is a jogging suit that plays different types of music to encourage the runner to go faster or slower. Then it sends an e-mail with information about the workout to the person's gym.

Some scientists believe that in the future people won't even need to carry cell phones or handheld computers. Instead we might type e-mail messages on fabric keyboards in our clothes, and make phone calls by talking into speakers on our shirt collars.

c Read the article again. Find examples of messages sent by intelligent clothing…

1 to the wearer.   2 to people nearby.   3 to people far away.

d Find a word in the article that means the following. (1) = paragraph number.

1 clothing (1): _____
2 people who steal (1): _____
3 information (2): _____
4 exercise (3): _____

e Work with a partner. Discuss the questions.

1 Which of these kinds of clothes would you like to wear?
2 How do you think intelligent clothing could be most useful to people?

15 Lifetime achievements

✔ Accomplishments and past events
✔ Present perfect

1 ▶ Reading

a Look at the photograph and read the first paragraph in the article. Who is this man?

b Read the rest of the article. Write one of the following questions in the space above each answer.

> What are your goals for the future?
> Are you afraid when you're on the trapeze?
> Are people surprised that you take so many risks?
> Why did you decide to take up the trapeze?

c Read the article again. Write T (true) or F (false).

1 Sam Keen is a professor at a university.
   _F_

2 He took up the trapeze when he was young.
   —

3 He believes that it is good to take risks.
   —

4 He believes that old people can do more than we think.
   —

5 He still has a lot of goals for the future.
   —

d Do you agree that "our society has a low opinion of what older people can do"?

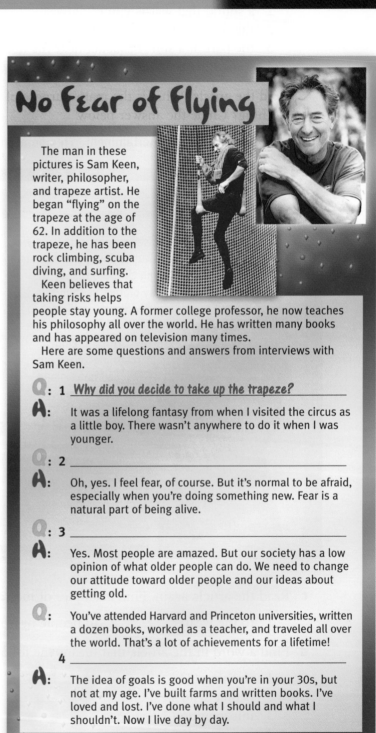

No Fear of Flying

The man in these pictures is Sam Keen, writer, philosopher, and trapeze artist. He began "flying" on the trapeze at the age of 62. In addition to the trapeze, he has been rock climbing, scuba diving, and surfing.

Keen believes that taking risks helps people stay young. A former college professor, he now teaches his philosophy all over the world. He has written many books and has appeared on television many times.

Here are some questions and answers from interviews with Sam Keen.

Q: 1 _Why did you decide to take up the trapeze?_

A: It was a lifelong fantasy from when I visited the circus as a little boy. There wasn't anywhere to do it when I was younger.

Q: 2 _____

A: Oh, yes. I feel fear, of course. But it's normal to be afraid, especially when you're doing something new. Fear is a natural part of being alive.

Q: 3 _____

A: Yes. Most people are amazed. But our society has a low opinion of what older people can do. We need to change our attitude toward older people and our ideas about getting old.

Q: You've attended Harvard and Princeton universities, written a dozen books, worked as a teacher, and traveled all over the world. That's a lot of achievements for a lifetime!

4 _____

A: The idea of goals is good when you're in your 30s, but not at my age. I've built farms and written books. I've loved and lost. I've done what I should and what I shouldn't. Now I live day by day.

2 ▸ Focus on Grammar

a Look at the chart. Find examples of the present perfect in the article on page 91.

b Choose the correct ending for the sentence. Circle *a* or *b*.

The present perfect describes…
a things that happened at a specific time in the past (we know when).
b things that happened at an unspecified time in the past (we don't know when).

Present perfect: Statements				
Affirmative (have + past participle)			**Negative (have + not + past participle)**	
I / You We / They He / She	**have** **have** **has**	**traveled** a lot. **written** books.	I / You We / They He / She	**have not** (haven't) **have not** **has not** (hasn't)	**traveled** a lot. **written** books.

Note: I have = I've   He has = he's
To form the past participle with regular verbs, add *-ed* to the base form.

c Here are some common irregular past participles. What are the base forms?

1 done ____*do*____   3 seen _____   5 broken _____
2 given _____   4 driven _____   6 flown _____

d Fill in the blanks using the present perfect of the verbs in parentheses.

1 *Steps to Life* is playing at the Royal. I __*haven't seen*__ (not see) that movie.
2 Cynthia's brother has a car but she _____ (not drive) it.
3 My young cousin _____ (break) his arm three times.
4 Thank you so much. You _____ (give) me a lot of help.
5 I _____ (do) this before, but I still can't remember how to do it.
6 The children are excited because they _____ (not fly) in an airplane.

3 ▸ *KnowHow*: Irregular verb forms

a Read these suggestions for learning irregular verb forms.

1 Write the base form on the front of a card, and the past simple and past participle forms on the back. Look at the cards frequently and test yourself. Work with a partner and test each other.
2 Make your own list of irregular verbs. Organize verbs that follow a similar pattern into groups, and learn them.
3 Use rhymes and mental images to help you remember. The more unusual, the better!

b Choose one of the suggestions to help you remember the irregular verb forms in this unit.

They ate and drank in a bank.

4 ► Vocabulary: Achievements

a Here are some different kinds of achievements. Which of these do you think is the most difficult to do?

run a marathon

start your own business

raise children

b Match each verb on the left with a phrase on the right.

1	write	*1c*	a	a medal, an award
2	appear	—	b	from college
3	win	—	c	a book, an article
4	travel	—	d	to fly, scuba dive, or swim
5	graduate	—	e	overseas, around the world
6	learn	—	f	in a movie, on television

c Work with a partner. Discuss the questions.

1 Which things in 4a and 4b have you done?
2 Which of these would you like to do?

5 ► In Conversation

AUDIO What has the astronaut done? Listen. Then read.

Interviewer: How many times have you flown in space?

Astronaut: Three times. The last time was a year ago.

Interviewer: Have you ever left the spacecraft?

Astronaut: Yes. I've gone on a space walk.

Interviewer: Really? When did you do that?

Astronaut: In 2002, on a mission to the Global Space Station.

Interviewer: What was it like?

Astronaut: It was an amazing experience!

6 ▶ Focus on Grammar

a Underline four questions in the conversation on page 93. Then circle *a* or *b* for each question below.

1 To ask about an experience at any time in someone's life, use…
   a the present perfect.   b the simple past.
2 To ask for details about a specific event, use…
   a the present perfect.   b the simple past.

Present perfect: Questions

Questions		*Answers*
How many times **have** you	**flown** in space?	Three times.
Have you (ever)	**won** a medal?	Yes, I **have**. / No, I **haven't**.
Has he / she	**written** a book?	Yes, he **has**. / No, he **hasn't**.

Note: To ask for details about a specific event, use the simple past.
When did you do that? —In 1998.
What was it like? —It was an amazing experience.

---

b **AUDIO** Look at the chart. Circle the correct phrase. Then listen and check your answers.

A: ¹(Have you ever visited / did you ever visit) the Art Museum?
B: Yes, ²(I have / I did).
A: When ³(have you gone / did you go) there?
B: A couple of months ago.
A: ⁴(Have you liked / Did you like) it?
B: Oh, yes.

c Work with a partner. Ask and answer questions. For each *yes* answer, ask at least two follow-up questions.

Example   A: *Have you ever ridden on a motorcycle?*
          B: *Oh, yes, of course.*
          A: *When was that?*
          B: *When I was about 19. My friend had a motorcycle. I rode with him.*
          A: *Did you like it?*
          B: *Yes, except when he rode too fast!*

▼ Help Desk

Ever = at any time

The word *never* is often used to make negative sentences.

*I've **never** climbed a mountain.*

Have you ever…
(ride) on a motorcycle?   (go) fishing?   (climb) a mountain?
(play) the lottery?   (win) anything?   (find) money in the street?
(sing) in public?   (be) to a wedding?   (give) blood?

d Do the activity again with a new partner.

7 ▶ Listening: Song

a Read the song. Try to fill in the blanks with the words below. What do you think it is about?

changed	friends	gone	living	lovers
think	remember	love	loved	

IN MY LIFE_____

There are places I'll ¹ *remember* all my life,
though some have ²_____
Some forever, not for better
Some have ³_____ and some remain
All these places had their moments
With lovers and ⁴_____ I still can recall
Some are dead and some are ⁵_____
In my life, I've ⁶_____ them all

But of all these friends and ⁷_____
There is no one compares with you
And these memories lose their meaning
When I think of love as something new
Though I know I'll never lose affection
For people and things that went before
I know I'll often stop and ⁸_____ about them
In my life, I'll ⁹_____ you more

b **AUDIO** Listen to the song and check your answers.

c Who is the song written to?

    an old friend   **an old lover**   **a new lover**

d What people and places will you always remember?

8 ▶ Speaking

a Think about your own experience. Make notes about the following:

  1 the most interesting place that you have visited
  2 the best celebration that you have ever had
  3 the most unusual person that you have met
  4 two things that you have done that you feel good about
  5 two things that you have not done but would like to do
  6 one thing that you have done and that you do not want to do again

b Work with a partner. Ask and answer questions about your experiences.

Example   A: *What's the most interesting place that you have visited?*
                B: *Well, I've been to India. I went there three years ago*
                   with my brother. We visited the Taj Mahal.
                   What about you?
                A: *The most interesting place I've been to is…*

> ▼ **Help Desk**
>
> *I've been to* (a place) means *I've visited* (a place).
>
> *I've been to India. I went there three years ago.*

9 ▶ Language in Action: Special occasions

a Look at the pictures. What would you say to the person in each situation? Choose one or more of the phrases below.

> **GREETINGS FOR SPECIAL OCCASIONS**
> ———————————————————————————
> • Good luck on your exam / in your new job / in your new home.
> • I hope you do well / win / feel better soon.
> • I'm sure you'll pass / be very happy.
> • Congratulations on your success / graduation!
> • Happy birthday / anniversary!
> • How wonderful / exciting!
> • I'm sorry you're not feeling well.

b Work with a partner. Act out a short conversation for each situation.

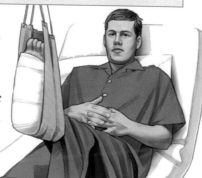

> Example   A: *I'm sorry you're not feeling well. I hope you feel better soon.*
> B: *Thank you.*

10 ▶ Writing

a Match the following message to one of the greeting cards below.

> **We've just heard the wonderful news. Congratulations, and welcome to little William!**

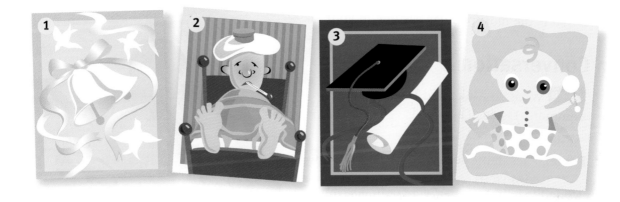

b Write a short message for each of the other three cards. Write them on three separate pieces of paper.

c Work with a partner. Exchange papers. Which message goes with which card?

16 Hobbies and habits

✔ Free time activities
✔ Auxiliaries + *too* / *either*; adverbs

1 ▶ Speaking

a Answer the questionnaire about free time. Fill in the first column in the chart.

What do you do in your free time?

Do you...	You	Person 1	Person 2
read magazines?			
watch old movies?			
play computer games?			
play an outdoor sport?			
watch sports on TV?			
play an instrument?			
play chess?			
paint or draw?			

b Ask two other people about their pastimes. Write the answers in the questionnaire. For every *Yes* answer, ask a follow-up question.

Example   A: *Do you read magazines?*
              B: *Yes, I do.*
              A: *What kind of magazines do you read?*
              B: *Sports magazines.*

c What is the most popular pastime in your class?

2 ▶ In Conversation

AUDIO What do Akiko and Daniel have in common? Listen. Then read.

Akiko: Do you read much?
Daniel: Yes, but I don't read books very much. Do you?
Akiko: No. I don't either. I read magazines.
Daniel: I do too. What kind of magazines do you like?
Akiko: Current affairs, mainly. I like *News Weekly*. Do you read that?
Daniel: I don't, but my wife does.

3 ▶ Focus on Grammar

a Look at the chart and answer the questions.

1 What do the short responses mean in each case?

Example *I do too. = I like to read magazines, too.*

2 Which word is used in negative responses: *too* or *either*?

Auxiliaries + *too / either*	
Statement	*Response*
I like to read magazines.	I **do too.**
I'm reading that book.	My wife **is too.**
We saw that movie.	We **did too.**
I'm not watching TV.	I'm **not either.**
I can't play chess.	I **can't either.**
I don't read the newspaper.	I **don't either,** but my husband **does.**

b Add a response to each of these statements. Use the word in parentheses and *too* or *either*.

1 I love art. (My sister)   *My sister does too.*
2 Philip and Marina rented that video. (We) _____
3 My sons don't play football. (My son)   _____
4 Grace can play chess. (Howard)   _____
5 I'm not using the computer. (I)   _____
6 I'm watching the game. (My cousin)   _____

c Fill in the blanks with *too*, *either*, or an auxiliary.

1 I went to the gym last night.   Really? I did *too*_____. But I didn't see you.
2 We didn't see the game last night.   I didn't _____, but Carter _____.
3 Do your friends play sports?   Yes. Most of them _____, but some _____.
4 I'm not going to the concert.   I'm not _____, but my cousin _____.

d Work with a partner. Talk about the results of the questionnaire on page 97.
Use auxiliaries and *too* or *either*.

Example *Amy reads magazines, and I do too.*

4 ▶ Writing

a Think about someone you know well. What interests and hobbies do you share? How are your interests different? Make notes about these two areas:

1 Sports and exercise
2 Music, TV, and movies

b Write about yourself and your friend. In the first paragraph, write about sports and exercise. In the second paragraph, write about music, TV, and movies.

Pat and I like different kinds of sports and exercise. Pat is more active than I am. She plays basketball and runs regularly.

As for music, TV, and movies, we are similar. Pat likes rock music, and I do too. We both enjoy movies and we love the theater. She doesn't watch TV, and I don't either.

5 ▶ Vocabulary: Sports and activities

a Look at the list of sports and activities. Which ones are in the pictures?

badminton	baseball	basketball	biking	diving	running
skateboarding	soccer	swimming	tennis	volleyball	skiing

b Put the activities into the following categories. (Some activities will go into more than one.)

on snow or in water	often alone	with a ball	with a bat or racket	on wheels
swimming				

c Look at the examples. Fill in the blanks with *play* or *go*.

We **play** soccer and chess.   Our neighbors often **go** camping.

Use _____ for a sport with a ball, or for a game with an opponent (chess, cards).
Use _____ + verb + *-ing* for other activities.

d Work with a partner. Say which activities you often, sometimes, or never do. Use *play* or *go*.

Example   *I never play badminton.*

6 ▶ *KnowHow*: Pronunciation of /s/ and /ʃ/

a **AUDIO** Listen to the words. Write 1 for the / s / sound and 2 for the / ʃ / sound.

Example   swim: _1_   dance: _1_   wash: _2_   action: _2_

1 soccer	__	3 sugar	__	5 sure	__	7 baseball	__
2 shopping	__	4 certainly	__	6 ocean	__	8 fashion	__

b **AUDIO** Listen and repeat the words. Practice the / s / and / ʃ / sounds.

7 Listening

a Can you find these parts of the body in the pictures?

legs	foot	shoulders
neck	head	stomach
heels	fingers	hands
arms	back	nose
eyes	mouth	knees

horseback riding

b **AUDIO** Listen. Circle the parts of the body above that you hear.

c **AUDIO** Listen again and fill in the blanks in the instructions.

Riding instructor:
1 Kick gently with *both legs.*
2 Keep _____ down. _____ your arms.

Yoga teacher:
3 _____ on the floor and cross _____.
   Breathe deeply.
4 Now rest _____ lightly on _____.

yoga

d How did you learn to swim, ride a bicycle, or drive?

8 Focus on Grammar

a Adverbs are used with verbs to describe how we do things. Look at the examples in the chart. Find two more examples in 7c.

Adverbs			
Regular (adjective + -ly)		**Irregular**	
careful	Move **carefully** in the water.	hard	Blow out **hard.**
deep	Breathe **deeply.**	fast	Don't drive too **fast.**
		good	You play really **well.**

Note: Change -y to i before -ly: *easily, happily*

b Complete the paragraph with words from the list.

perfectly   hard   carefully   loudly   quickly

My son is a great soccer player. He runs ¹_____ because soccer is a fast game. He usually kicks the ball, but sometimes he hits it ²_____ with his head. The goalie has to watch the ball ³_____ when my son is near the goal. When he kicks the ball ⁴_____, it goes into the net and I shout, "GOAL!" very ⁵_____.

9 ▶ Language in Action: Instructions

a AUDIO How many instructions does Ken give? Listen. Then read.

Ken: OK. First, take the cap off.
Ali: OK.
Ken: Then you look through this little window here. Can you see?
Ali: No…Oh, now I can!
Ken: It focuses automatically.
Ali: Wow! That's great. What's this button?
Ken: Don't press that! It's for the battery.
Ali: Oh, sorry.
Ken: Now, just press this red button when you're ready. But don't press it too hard.
Ali: OK. I'm ready.

b Look at the box. Check the expressions that Ken uses.

GIVING INSTRUCTIONS
__ (OK.) First, (you)…
— Now…
__ Then…   / __ Next…   / __ After that,…
__ Finally,…
__ That's it.   / __ That's right.

▼ **Help Desk**

Use the **simple present** to **explain** how to do something:

You look through this little window.

Use the **imperative** to **tell** someone to do something. The imperative is more direct.

Don' t press that button! Press the red one.

c Work with a partner. Number the steps below 1 to 4. Give instructions using words from the box above.

1 __ Bend your knees.
   __ Bring your arms up over your head.
   __ Push off from the side.
   _1_ Stand at the side of the pool.

2 __ Pedal hard.
   __ Put one foot on the pedal.
   __ Sit on the seat.
   __ Push off with the other foot.

d Work with a partner. Choose one or more of the following activities, or use your own ideas. Explain how to do it.

use a camera   use a skateboard   swim   get on a horse

10 ▸ Reading

a Look at the pictures. What do you think of the cars on this page?

b Read the article. Which car is not illustrated?

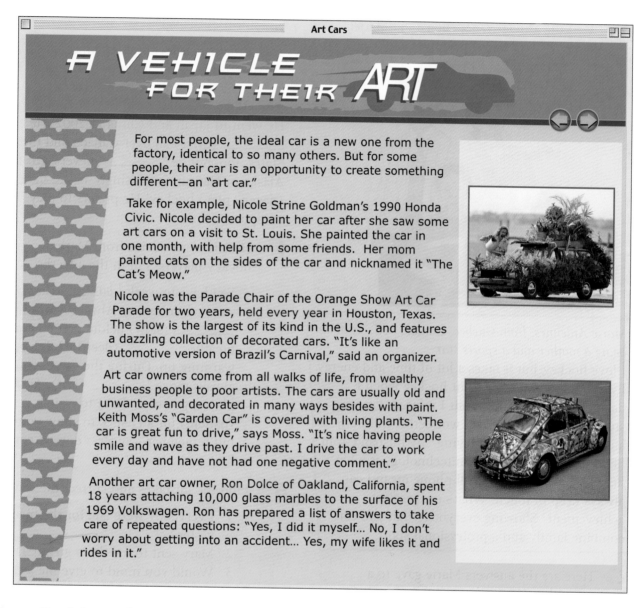

Art Cars

A VEHICLE FOR THEIR ART

For most people, the ideal car is a new one from the factory, identical to so many others. But for some people, their car is an opportunity to create something different—an "art car."

Take for example, Nicole Strine Goldman's 1990 Honda Civic. Nicole decided to paint her car after she saw some art cars on a visit to St. Louis. She painted the car in one month, with help from some friends. Her mom painted cats on the sides of the car and nicknamed it "The Cat's Meow."

Nicole was the Parade Chair of the Orange Show Art Car Parade for two years, held every year in Houston, Texas. The show is the largest of its kind in the U.S., and features a dazzling collection of decorated cars. "It's like an automotive version of Brazil's Carnival," said an organizer.

Art car owners come from all walks of life, from wealthy business people to poor artists. The cars are usually old and unwanted, and decorated in many ways besides with paint. Keith Moss's "Garden Car" is covered with living plants. "The car is great fun to drive," says Moss. "It's nice having people smile and wave as they drive past. I drive the car to work every day and have not had one negative comment."

Another art car owner, Ron Dolce of Oakland, California, spent 18 years attaching 10,000 glass marbles to the surface of his 1969 Volkswagen. Ron has prepared a list of answers to take care of repeated questions: "Yes, I did it myself... No, I don't worry about getting into an accident... Yes, my wife likes it and rides in it."

c Read the article again. Find and correct four more content errors in this summary.

Most art cars are ^*not* new cars, and the people who own them decorate them in the same way. Many show their cars at the Art Car Parade in Brazil. It's the smallest of its kind in the U.S. Sometimes it takes years to decorate a car. For example, Ron Dolce took ten years to decorate his. Everyone's art car is different!

d Do people decorate cars or other vehicles where you live? How?

Units 13–16 Review

Grammar

1 Read the article. What choice did Marie make? What kind of person is she?

Marie Ardennes, from Quebec, Canada, tells us about being a mother and a sports star.
I love hockey, but it takes a lot of time and energy. Everyone wanted me to quit hockey when I decided to raise a family, but I refused. I'm very stubborn. Now I have two wonderful children, and I've never stopped playing. My husband Tom helps me a lot, and modern technology is a big help too. My pager and cell phone mean I can always keep in touch. What's my greatest achievement? Showing everybody that you can combine family and a professional sport.

2 Here are the answers Marie gave to a journalist. What were the questions?

1 Who _taught you to play hockey_____?
My brothers taught me to play hockey.
2 How often _____?
I play hockey every day.
3 Who _____?
My friend Susan introduced me to my husband, Tom.
4 Who _____?
I admire successful women.

3 Read the passage about Marie's husband Tom and fill in the blanks with the present perfect form of the verbs.

Tom Ardennes is a computer expert and a writer. He started his own computer business in 2000. He ¹_____ (write) three books. He ²_____ (travel) all over the world to talk about his books. He went to Japan and China in 2002. He ³_____ (drive) all over Canada and the United States, too, but he ⁴_____ (never / go) to Alaska or Hawaii. Surprisingly, he ⁵_____ (never / play) hockey! He prefers to play computer games.

4 Here is some advice from Marie for young hockey players. Fill in the adverbs.

You have to work ¹ _hard____ (hard) to succeed in hockey. Always warm up ²_____ (slow) before you play, and breathe ³_____ (deep) while you are warming up. During the game, you should always move ⁴_____ (fast). As a new player, you often have to wait ⁵_____ (patient) for a chance to show your skills, but remember—success doesn't come ⁶_____ (easy)!

5 Find the mistakes and correct the sentences.

1 Everybody were late for the meeting yesterday.
2 Mary sent to me these great CDs.
3 Would you mind to give me a call tomorrow morning?
4 Marie and Tom have met in 1997.

6 Finish the sentences to make predictions.

1 In the future, I'm sure that computers will _____.
2 In ten years, I definitely won't _____.
3 After class, I might _____.
4 In the future, public transportation might not _____.

103

Vocabulary

7 The words in **bold** are in the wrong sentences. Put them in the right ones.

1 I love to send and receive **Internet**—it's better than writing letters.

2 Marie needs her **VCR** to keep in touch with her children when she's away from home.

3 I found a **personal computer** on my answering machine from Tom.

4 You can buy things and find information on the **message**.

5 We recorded the hockey match on our **e-mail**.

6 Having a **pager** at home is useful for writing letters and playing games.

8 Write two true sentences about things you've done in the past and two sentences about what you plan to do in the future. Use the ideas below and / or your own ideas.

**vacation   college   medal / award
movie / TV   a book   a new job   a family**

Example   *I have graduated from college.
I would like to run a marathon.*

_____

_____

_____

_____

9 Cross out the word that doesn't work in each sentence. Can you find others that work?

1 I need a new _____ for my computer.
keyboard   mouse   printer   shoulder

2 In yoga class we _____ a lot.
sit   browse   stand   bend

3 Bill is a great friend. He's very _____.
optimistic   honest   lazy   reliable

4 Jeff likes to _____ new software on his computer.
install   win   search for   download

Recycling Center

10 Complete the conversations with the correct forms of the verbs.

1 **Ella:** What _____ (you / do) yesterday?

Rose: I _____ (go) shopping with some friends. We _____ (have) a really good time, but I _____ (spend) too much money!

2 **Abby:** Hey, Tom, what _____ (you / do) now?

Tom: I _____ (work) on the annual report. Why?

Abby: I _____ (want) to go out to eat. _____ (you / want) to go?

3 **Yung:** What _____ (you / plan) to do next year?

Han: I _____ (like) to study in California. What about you?

Yung: I _____ (want) to get an interesting job. I _____ (be) tired of studying all the time!

Fun Spot

Put the letters in order to make words about personality. Write the words in the squares.

1 T H O E N S

2 B S N O B T R U

3 Z L Y A

4 L E F Y N I R D

5 D I K N

Now put the letters in the circles in order to make another word.

_ _ _ _ _ _ _ _

Keep on talking!

UNIT
1 Neighborhood party: Student A

(For B's part of this activity, go to page 107.)

Work with a partner. **A**, you are at a neighborhood barbecue. Your friend Diana Avilar invited you. You know some of the other people, but not all of them. Ask **B** questions to find out information about the other people.

Name	Age	Job	Relationship
Diana Avilar	59	doctor	Leo's wife
Simon Bolton	55	business person	Leo's colleague
Elizabeth James	62	doctor	Diana's colleague
Paul Watkins	7	no job	April's son
Dave Wilson			
Leo Avilar			
Daniel Avilar			
April Watkins			

UNIT
2 Vacation plans: Pair A

(For B's part of this activity, go to page 107.)

1 Work in groups of four (Pair A and Pair B). The group wants to travel to Paris and stay for one week. Each pair has different information about flight and hotel packages. **Pair A**, look at the information on this page. Ask **Pair B** questions about trips 3 and 4 and fill in the information.

Trip 1	Trip 2
leaves 6:15 a.m.	leaves 10:30 a.m.
takes 12.5 hours (2 stops)	takes 15 hours (2 stops)
costs $1,095 per person	costs $2,025 per person
includes 2 meals a day, one day travel pass	includes breakfast, free tour
Trip 3	**Trip 4**
leaves _____	leaves _____
takes _____ hours (2 stops)	takes _____ hours (3 stops)
costs _____ per person	costs _____ per person
includes _____	includes _____

2 Discuss the options in your group and choose one trip together. Which trip did you choose? Why?

3 ▶ What do you do for fun?

1 Work with a partner. Answer the questions and compare your answers. Do you do the same kinds of things? What unusual activities do you do? Now compare the results of the survey with the class.

ENTERTAINMENT QUESTIONNAIRE	
1 Movies	*4 Outdoor activities*
–how often?	–how often?
–favorite actor / actress?	–what type?
–favorite movie?	–organized / team sports?
2 Books	*5 Restaurants*
–how many a month?	–how often?
–buy or borrow from library?	–what kind?
–favorite author?	–what food?
3 Television	*6 Other activities*
–how many hours a week?	–how often?
–what kind of shows?	–what type?
–favorite program?	–any classes / clubs?

2 You and your partner want to open a new business in your city. Based on the results of the class survey, what type of business would you open? Why?

a movie theater	a bookstore	an electronics store
a sports store	a restaurant	(other) _____

5 ▶ Waiting for the train: Student A

(For B's part of this activity, go to page 109.)

Work with a partner. A, you arrive at the station at 7:00 a.m., and you'll catch another train at 2:00 p.m. Read the suggestions below and decide on four things you want to do while you wait for your train. Go to the information desk and ask B where the places are and what time they open.

have breakfast	buy a book
get money	shop for a gift
read a newspaper	buy a CD
eat lunch	get a map
drink a cup of coffee	buy a souvenir

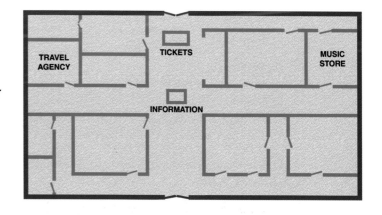

Example
A: *Where can I buy a souvenir?*
B: *At the gift shop.*
A: *Where is it?*
B: *Next to the music store.*
A: *What time does it open?*
B: *At…*

UNIT 1 Neighborhood party: Student B

(For A's part of this activity, go to page 105).

Work with a partner. **B**, you are at a neighborhood barbecue. Your friend Jorge Avilar invited you. You know some of the people, but not all of them. Ask **A** questions to find out information about the other people.

Name	Age	Job	Relationship
Diana Avilar			
Simon Bolton			
Elizabeth James			
Paul Watkins			
Dave Wilson	57	lawyer	Diana and Leo's neighbor
Leo Avilar	59	business person	Diana's husband
Daniel Avilar	29	pilot	Leo and Diana's son
April Watkins	32	writer	Leo and Diana's daughter

UNIT 2 Vacation plans: Pair B

(For A's part of this activity, go to page 105.)

1 Work in groups of four (Pair A and Pair B). The group wants to travel to Paris and stay for one week. Each pair has different information about flight and hotel packages. **Pair B**, look at the information on this page. Ask Pair A questions about trips 1 and 2 and fill in the information.

Trip 1	Trip 2
leaves _____	leaves _____
takes _____ hours (2 stops)	takes _____ hours (2 stops)
costs _____ per person	costs _____ per person
includes _____	includes _____
Trip 3	**Trip 4**
leaves 5:45 a.m.	leaves 2:30 p.m.
takes 11.5 hours (2 stops)	takes 15 hours (3 stops)
costs $1,450 per person	costs $1,950 per person
includes 2 meals a day, free car for one day	includes breakfast, free tour, 1 free museum pass

2 Discuss the options in your group and choose one trip together. Which trip did you choose? Why?

UNIT
4 **New office space**

1 Work with a partner. The staff of a small magazine is moving to a new office. Look at the plan of the office below and decide how to arrange it to meet the needs of the people listed. You can add portable walls.

Name	Position	Needs / wants
Ed Baker	President	He needs a corner office with a window, a desk, a sofa, a table, and chairs for meetings.
Carol Abdul	Editor	She needs a desk, a comfortable chair for guests, and tables for two computers. She likes to be near other people.
David Monsour	Assistant to editor	He needs to be near the editor's office. He needs a large desk and filing cabinets. He likes plants and natural light.
Anna Song	Receptionist	She needs to be near an entrance. She is allergic to plants.
Carrie Anders and Paul Davis	Design staff	They need to share a large office with lots of light. They each need a large work table.
Melanie Joseph	Sales manager	She needs a large desk and filing cabinets. She likes a quiet work space.

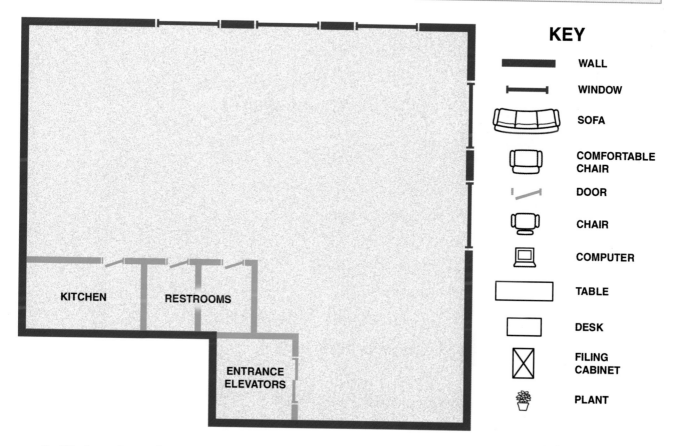

2 Work with another pair. Compare your office designs.

Waiting for the train: Student B

(For A's part of this activity, go to page 106.)

Work with a partner. **B**, you work at the information desk at the station. Answer the questions A asks. Give suggestions.

Place	Hours	Place	Hours
Travel agency	10 a.m.–8 p.m.	Gift shop	8 a.m.–8 p.m.
Restaurant	11 a.m.–8 p.m.	Music store	10 a.m.–7 p.m.
Newsstand	8 a.m.–10 p.m.	Women's boutique	10 a.m.–6 p.m.
Coffee shop	open 24 hours	Bank	9 a.m.–6 p.m.
Bookstore	closed for renovations		

Time capsule

1 Work in small groups. Decide what items to put in a time capsule. Choose items that best describe what life is like now where you live. Discuss different ideas for each category and decide together what to include.

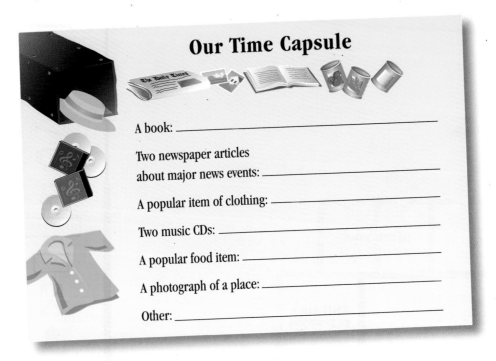

Our Time Capsule

A book: _____

Two newspaper articles about major news events: _____

A popular item of clothing: _____

Two music CDs: _____

A popular food item: _____

A photograph of a place: _____

Other: _____

2 Pretend it's the future, 100 years from now. Exchange "time capsules" with another group. Describe what life was like in the past for the other group.

UNIT
7 In the kitchen: Student A

(For B's part of this activity, go to page 111.)

A, you and your partner want to make gazpacho, a cold soup from Spain. Each of you has part of the recipe. Look at the list of ingredients and ask B questions to complete the recipe. You don't need to use all the ingredients.

<u>Ingredients</u>:

broccoli	tomatoes	red peppers	green peppers
onions	rice	carrots	chicken
butter	eggs	lemon juice	orange juice

Example
A: *How much broccoli do we need?* —B: *We don't need any broccoli.*
A: *How many tomatoes do we need?* —B: *We need...*

Recipe: Gazpacho

_____   1 can tomato juice   1 tablespoon cooking oil

1 cucumber   _____   _____

_____   _____   1/4 teaspoon pepper

1/4 teaspoon salt   2 cloves garlic   _____

Cut the vegetables into small pieces. In a large bowl mix the vegetables and all of the other ingredients. Cover and chill for two hours. Serve cold. Makes 6–8 bowls.

UNIT
8 Find someone who...

1 Go around your class and find someone who did each of the things listed. Write the name of the person. Ask questions to find out more details.

    Example A: Did you visit another country last year?
               B: Yes, I did.
               A: Where did you go?

Find someone who...
1 visited another country last year _____
2 had a job as a teenager _____
3 went to an exhibit last month _____
4 went to a sports event last month _____
5 could play a musical instrument at age 5 _____

6 was a student last year _____
7 went rock climbing last year _____
8 climbed a mountain this year _____
9 lived in another country as a child _____
10 found or won some money last month _____

2 Report to the class. How many people did you find for each item?

UNIT 7

In the kitchen: Student B

(For A's part of this activity, go to page 110.)

B, you and your partner want to make gazpacho, a cold soup from Spain. Each of you has part of the recipe. Look at the list of ingredients and ask A questions to complete the recipe. You don't need to use all the ingredients.

Ingredients:

crackers	apples	salt	pepper
potatoes	mushrooms	cucumbers	garlic
oil	beans	tomato juice	water

Example
B: *How much water do we need?* —A: *We don't need any water.*
B: *How many cucumbers do we need?* —A: *We need…*

Recipe: Gazpacho
6 tomatoes
_____   _____
_____   1 green pepper   1 red pepper
2 small onions   4 carrots
_____   _____
                  1 tablespoon lemon juice

Cut the vegetables into small pieces. In a large bowl mix the vegetables and all of the other ingredients. Cover and chill for two hours. Serve cold. Makes 6–8 bowls.

UNIT 9

The best place to live

1 Work in pairs. Imagine that you both want to spend a year on the island of Rodanor. (This is an imaginary place.) Look at the information about the four cities and compare them. Then decide together where you want to live.

2 Work with another pair. Tell which city you chose and why.

RODANOR

Qualities	Amberon	Portelle	Triville	Bolano
exciting	◆◆◆	◆◆	◆◆◆	◆◆◆◆
noisy	◆	◆◆◆◆	◆	◆◆◆
expensive	◆◆◆	◆◆	◆◆◆◆	◆◆◆◆
busy	◆◆	◆◆◆◆	◆◆◆	◆◆◆
warm	◆	◆◆◆	◆	◆◆
good transportation	◆◆◆◆	◆◆◆◆	◆◆◆	◆◆
museums / galleries	◆◆◆	◆◆	◆◆◆◆	◆◆◆
natural beauty	◆◆◆	◆◆	◆◆◆◆	◆◆
live music / theater	◆◆	◆◆◆	◆◆	◆◆◆◆

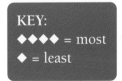

KEY:
◆◆◆◆ = most
◆ = least

UNIT 10 ▸ On the job

1 Play in groups of three. Use one marker for each person and one die.
2 Roll the die and move that number of spaces in any direction where spaces connect.
3 When you land on a space, read the clue and respond.
4 If your answer is correct, write your initials in the space and wait for your next turn. If it's wrong, leave the space blank.
5 If you land on a space with initials filled in, stay there and wait for your next turn.
6 Continue until all of the spaces are filled. The student with the most spaces wins.

UNIT
11 **What's your style?**

1 Fill in the questionnaire.

Shopping Questionnaire

1 What kind of clothes do you wear for work or school? (Circle one)
   very formal   pretty formal   pretty casual   very casual

2 What do you wear on weekends or days off?
   _____

3 Which of the following do you wear regularly? (Circle one or more)
   a hat   a tie   a scarf   boots   sneakers   sunglasses

4 Do you wear jewelry (rings, earrings, necklaces)? Why or why not?
   _____

5 What do you wear on special occasions?
   _____

6 What clothing are you most comfortable in?
   _____

7 What item of clothing would you most like to have?
   _____

8 How do you feel about shopping for clothes? (Circle one)
   I always dislike it.   I usually dislike it.
   I usually enjoy it.   I always enjoy it.

2 Work in small groups. Compare your answers to the questionnaire. How are you similar?
   How are you different?

UNIT
12 **Community planning**

1 Work in small groups. Your group has $100,000 to spend on projects for yourselves and the community. Decide which projects you will do and how you are going to spend the money. Choose from the ideas below.

Activity	Cost
• start a community English library	$40,000
• organize a free concert	$20,000
• improve a local playground	$60,000
• organize a community clean-up project	$10,000
• take a class trip to Europe	$50,000
• start a child-care center	$70,000
• start an animal hospital	$30,000

2 Report your plans to the class and explain your choices.

UNIT
13 **Problems and solutions**

1 Work in pairs. Look at the pictures and describe the problem in each picture. Then discuss the best advice to solve the problem.

2 Compare solutions in class and vote on the best solution to each problem.

14 ▶ Travel necessities

1 Work with a partner. A friend is taking a solo bike trip across the country. He or she wants your help to decide on <u>five</u> items to take from the list. Decide why the items would be useful (or not).

a map   small tent
video camera   cell phone
water bottle   laptop computer
dried food   books
raincoat and hat
portable CD player and CDs
drawing paper and pencils

2 Compare your items with the class. Did you choose the same items for the same reasons?

15 ▶ Are you adventurous?

1 Work in small groups. Think of something exciting or unusual that you have done. Use the ideas below and your own ideas. Take turns asking the group, *Have you ever…?* Each person who has done it (including yourself) gets one point. After the group has asked 12–15 questions, total your points.

read an interesting book?   traveled to an interesting place?
tried an unusual sport?   eaten some unusual food?
met a famous person?   won an unusual award?
attended an exciting event?   had an exciting or unusual job?

Examples *Have you ever read* War and Peace?
Have you ever been to Timbuktu?

2 Analyze your results.

2–4 points:	Try to add some excitement to your life by taking up a new sport or traveling.
5–8 points:	You have done some fun things. Keep up the good work!
9–11 points:	Congratulations! You live an exciting life.
12+ points:	You are very adventurous and interesting. But, be careful! Don't try anything dangerous!

16 ▶ Evening classes

1 Work with a partner. Look at the descriptions of the people and the list of evening classes. Discuss which class or classes you think each person would be interested in and why.

Name and Description	Interests and lifestyle	Name and Description	Interests and lifestyle
 Anna Nguyen – 36 lawyer	She has a very busy lifestyle. She was athletic as a girl, but now she gets little exercise. Anna enjoys classical music and visiting art galleries.	 Anastasia Ablaro – 24 department store clerk	She enjoys fashion and interior decorating, gardening, and dancing. She has very little free time or spare money.
 David Tenaglia – 25 taxi driver	He likes cars, watches sports on TV, and is interested in journalism. He would like to travel to other countries.	 Andrew Jones – 60 retired engineer	He enjoys cooking, going for walks, and collecting works of art and antiques. Andrew has some health problems and needs to get more exercise.

2 Compare your decisions with the class. Did you have the same suggestions?

EVENING CLASSES AT THE COMMUNITY CENTER

BEGINNING GERMAN CONVERSATION
Learn the basics of German conversation in a relaxed atmosphere, and experience German food, culture, and traditions, too.
Mon & Wed 5–6:30

FLAMENCO
Learn the traditional dance of Spain.
No experience needed.
Tues 6–8

JOURNAL WRITING WORKSHOP
See your life in a new way by writing down your experiences. Explore journals by other writers.
Mon & Fri 7–8

CONTAINER GARDENING
Learn to create beautiful pots and planters and how to choose and combine plants.
Wed 7–9

TAI CHI
Experience the physical and mental benefits of this ancient exercise.
Mon & Wed 6–7

DOLLAR-WISE DECORATING
Learn to brighten up your rooms without spending a lot. Make the most of what you have.
Thurs 7–9

BASIC DRAWING
Learn the basics of figure and landscape drawing.
Tues & Thurs 6–7

Vocabulary Reference

Abbreviation Key

n. - noun
v. - verb
adj. - adjective
pron. - pronoun
adv. - adverb
prep. - preposition

This section brings together key words and expressions from each unit. Use *Word for Word* to note down other important words that you want to remember.

Common Word Groups

Numbers *(n.)*

zero (oh)
one
two
three
four
five
six
seven
eight
nine
ten
eleven
twelve
thirteen
fourteen
fifteen
sixteen
seventeen
eighteen
nineteen
twenty
twenty-one
twenty-two
twenty-three
twenty-four
twenty-five
twenty-six
twenty-seven
twenty-eight
twenty-nine
thirty
forty
fifty
sixty
seventy
eighty
ninety
one hundred

Ordinal Numbers *(adj.)*

first
second
third
fourth
fifth
sixth
seventh
eighth
ninth
tenth
eleventh
twelfth
thirteenth
fourteenth
fifteenth
sixteenth
seventeenth
eighteenth
nineteenth
twentieth
twenty-first
twenty-second
thirtieth
thirty-first

Days *(n.)*

Sunday
Monday
Tuesday
Wednesday
Thursday
Friday
Saturday

Months *(n.)*

January
February
March
April
May
June
July
August
September
October
November
December

Unit 1: Meeting and greeting

aunt (*n.*)
boyfriend (*n.*)
brother (*n.*)
brother-in-law (*n.*)
capital (*n.*)
child / children (*n.*)
colleague (*n.*)
cousin (*n.*)
daughter (*n.*)
family (*n.*)
father (*n.*)
first name (*n.*)
friend (*n.*)
from (*prep.*)
girlfriend (*n.*)
grandfather (*n.*)
grandmother (*n.*)
husband (*n.*)
last name (*n.*)
live (*v.*)

man / men (*n.*)
Miss (*n.*)
mother (*n.*)
Mr. (*n.*)
Mrs. (*n.*)
Ms. (*n.*)
near (*prep.*)
neighbor (*n.*)
nephew (*n.*)
niece (*n.*)
parent (*n.*)
person / people (*n.*)
sister (*n.*)
sister-in-law (*n.*)
son (*n.*)
student (*n.*)
uncle (*n.*)
wedding (*n.*)
wife (*n.*)
woman / women (*n.*)

Expressions
Good morning.
Good night.
Goodbye.
How are you?
I'm fine, thanks.
My name is….
Nice to meet you.
Really?
See you tomorrow.
Thank you.
This is….
What about you?
Where are you from?
You're welcome.

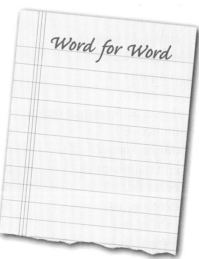

Unit 2: From here to there

airplane (*n.*)
bicycle (*n.*)
bike stand (*n.*)
bored (*adj.*)
bus (*n.*)
cable car (*n.*)
car (*n.*)
city (*n.*)
comfortable (*adj.*)
different (*adj.*)
do (*v.*)
downtown (*adj.*)
drive (*v.*)
early (*adj.*)
enjoy (*v.*)
evening (*n.*)
every (*adj.*)
fast (*adj.*)
ferry (*n.*)
finish (*v.*)
free (*adj.*)
get up (*v.*)

go (*v.*)
happy (*adj.*)
have (*v.*)
home (*n.*)
hungry (*adj.*)
job (*n.*)
late (*adj.*)
leave (*v.*)
like (*v.*)
listen (*v.*)
many (*adj.*)
money (*n.*)
morning (*n.*)
motorcycle (*n.*)
music (*n.*)
nervous (*adj.*)
newspaper (*n.*)
popular (*adj.*)
practical (*adj.*)
program (*n.*)
public transportation (*n.*)

read (*v.*)
relax (*v.*)
return (*v.*)
ride (*n., v.*)
sad (*adj.*)
school (*n.*)
sit (*v.*)
sleep (*v.*)
slow (*adj.*)
stay (*v.*)
subway (*n.*)
take (*v.*)
taxi (*n.*)
teach (*v.*)
thirsty (*adj.*)
tired (*adj.*)
train (*n.*)
trip (*n.*)
unusual (*adj.*)
use (*v.*)
walk (*n., v.*)
watch (*v.*)

work (*n., v.*)

Expressions
Thank you very much.
Excuse me.

Unit 3: On the go

a lot (*n., adv.*)
always (*adv.*)
amusement park (*n.*)
art exhibit (*n.*)
athlete (*n.*)
baseball (*n.*)
busy (*adj.*)
class (*n.*)
classical music (*n.*)
clothes (*n.*)
computer (*n.*)
concert (*n.*)
dance performance (*n.*)
dinner (*n.*)
during (*prep.*)
entertainment (*n.*)
event (*n.*)
exercise (*v.*)
exhibit (*n.*)
festival (*n.*)
get together with (*v.*)

go out (*v.*)
go shopping (*v.*)
gym (*n.*)
hardly ever (*adv.*)
indoors (*adv.*)
jazz (*n.*)
live music (*n.*)
meet (*v.*)
movies (*n.*)
museum (*n.*)
never (*adv.*)
note (*n.*)
not much (*adv.*)
often (*adv.*)
outdoors (*adv.*)
park (*n.*)
pattern (*n.*)
performance (*n.*)
play (*n., v.*)
recover (*v.*)
restaurant (*n.*)

rhythm (*n.*)
rock concert (*n.*)
sometimes (*adv.*)
theater (*n.*)
usually (*adv.*)
visit (*v.*)
write (*v.*)

Expressions

Would you like
 to…?
Let's….
How about…?
I'm sorry.
That sounds good.

Word for Word

Unit 4: Personal spaces

across from (*prep.*)
armchair (*n.*)
arrangement (*n.*)
balance (*v.*)
balcony (*n.*)
beach (*n.*)
beautiful (*adj.*)
bed (*n.*)
bedroom (*n.*)
behind (*prep.*)
between (*prep.*)
blinds (*n.*)
block (*v.*)
book (*n.*)
bookcase (*n.*)
chair (*n.*)
clean (*adj.*)
coffee table (*n.*)
corner (*n.*)
cut up (*v.*)

desk (*n.*)
dining room (*n.*)
door (*n.*)
edge (*n.*)
energy (*n.*)
environment (*n.*)
exchange (*n., v.*)
Feng Shui (*n.*)
file cabinet (*n.*)
furniture (*n.*)
garden (*n.*)
glass (*adj.*)
house (*n.*)
in (*prep.*)
in front of (*prep.*)
kitchen (*n.*)
lamp (*n.*)
line (*n.*)
living room (*n.*)
location (*n.*)

metal (*n.*)
move (*v.*)
neat (*adj.*)
next to (*prep.*)
office (*n.*)
on (*prep.*)
open (*adj.*)
over (*prep.*)
philosophy (*n.*)
picture (*n.*)
place (*n.*)
plant (*n.*)
put (*v.*)
quiet (*adj.*)
refrigerator (*n.*)
relaxing (*adj.*)
rent (*v.*)
room (*n.*)
rounded (*adj.*)
rug (*n.*)

sharp (*adj.*)
sink (*n.*)
sofa (*n.*)
stove (*n.*)
table (*n.*)
television (*n.*)
traditional (*adj.*)
tree house (*n.*)
under (*prep.*)
unhappy (*adj.*)
unlucky (*adj.*)
view (*n.*)
wall (*n.*)
window (*n.*)
wooden (*adj.*)

Unit 5: Public places

airport (n.)
available (adj.)
baggage (n.)
baggage claim (n.)
bank (n.)
birthday present (n.)
buy (v.)
canceled (adj.)
cash machine (n.)
celebrate (v.)
coffee shop (n.)
cold (adj.)
complex (n.)
corridor (n.)
customs (n.)
department store (n.)
employ (v.)
employee (n.)
escalator (n.)
explore (v.)
flight (n.)

freezing (adj.)
gate (n.)
go up/down (v.)
golf course (n.)
hotel (n.)
information desk (n.)
magazine (n.)
mall (n.)
map (n.)
miniature (adj.)
movie theater (n.)
outside (adv.)
parking garage (n.)
parking space (n.)
post office (n.)
public telephone (n.)
restroom (n.)
sandwich (n.)
shop (n., v.)
size (n.)
skating rink (n.)

snack bar (n.)
store (n.)
suitcase (n.)
swimming pool (n.)
telephone (n.)
tourist (n.)
weather (n.)
world (n.)

Expressions
What are you
doing here?

Unit 6: Now and then

alone (adj.)
answer (n., v.)
arrive at (v.)
backwards (adv.)
breakfast (n.)
call (v.)
clock (n.)
crazy (adj.)
dress (v.)
electricity (n.)
establish (v.)
fashionable (adj.)
forwards (adv.)
industrialization (n.)
interview (n.)
invent (v.)
journal (n.)
journalist (n.)
lack (n.)
local time (n.)
lunch (n.)

mechanical (adj.)
meeting (n.)
moon (n.)
neighboring (adj.)
network (n.)
news (n.)
normal (adj.)
old (adj.)
on time (adv.)
own (v.)
photograph (n.)
problem (n.)
province (n.)
railroad (n.)
report (n.)
reset (a clock) (v.)
set (a clock) (v.)
simple (adj.)
standard (n.)
sun (n.)
system (n.)

tell (v.)
time (n.)
time management (n.)
time zone (n.)
TV station (n.)
uncomplicated (adj.)
useful (adj.)
village (n.)
watch (n.)
wait (v.)

Unit 7: Food for thought

adult (n.)
allergic (adj.)
amount (n.)
apple (n.)
beans (n.)
bowl (n.)
bread (n.)
broccoli (n.)
butter (n.)
can (n.)
candy (n.)
carrot (n.)
cereal (n.)
cheese (n.)
coffee (n.)
colorful (adj.)
cookies (n.)
crackers (n.)
dessert (n.)
dictionary (n.)

diet (n.)
dried fruit (n.)
drink (v.)
egg (n.)
encourage (v.)
exercise (n., v.)
fish (n.)
food (n.)
fresh (adj.)
fruit (n.)
glass (n.)
grammar (n.)
ingredient (n.)
juice (n.)
kid (n.)
label (n.)
lettuce (n.)
machine (n.)
meaning (n.)
meat (n.)

menu (n.)
milk (n.)
mineral water (n.)
order (v.)
overweight (adj.)
pasta (n.)
pedal (v.)
pepper (n.)
percent (n.)
pizza (n.)
potato (n.)
poultry (n.)
pronounce (v.)
pronunciation (n.)
recognize (v.)
regular (adj.)
regularly (adj.)
research (n.)
rice (n.)
right (adj.)

salmon (n.)
salt (n.)
scientist (n.)
seafood (n.)
shopping cart (n.)
sleep (n., v.)
slice (n.)
snack (n.)
soda (n.)
soup (n.)
stress (n.)
sugar (n.)
supermarket (n.)
tomato (n.)
vegetable (n.)
vegetarian (n.)
water (n.)

Unit 8: Read all about it

accept (v.)
after (prep.)
amazing (adj.)
antique store (n.)
arrest (v.)
awful (adj.)
bad (adj.)
beat (v.)
block (n.)
branch (n.)
break into (v.)
burglary (n.)
cast (v.)
climb (v.)
come back (v.)
drown (v.)
find (v.)
frightening (adj.)
garage (n.)
gift (n.)

glasses (n.)
good (adj.)
great (adj.)
happen (v.)
headline (n.)
ice (n.)
incredible (adj.)
investigate (v.)
laugh (v.)
locked (adj.)
missing (adj.)
neighborhood (n.)
police (n.)
price (n.)
pull (v.)
record (n.)
reward (n.)
rich (adj.)
salesperson (n.)
scary (adj.)

shade (n.)
sign (n.)
silhouette (n.)
sore (adj.)
squirrel (n.)
steal (v.)
stolen (adj.)
strange (adj.)
surprising (adj.)
sweater (n.)
swim (v.)
terrible (adj.)
vase (n.)
weird (adj.)
wonderful (adj.)
yard (n.)
yell (v.)

Word for Word

Unit 9: Cities and sites

atmosphere (n.)
big (adj.)
cheap (adj.)
climate (n.)
cloudy (adj.)
coast (n.)
conclusion (n.)
connection (n.)
convenient (adj.)
country (n.)
dangerous (adj.)
dark (adj.)
dirty (adj.)
exciting (adj.)
expensive (adj.)
fight (n.)
friendly (adj.)
grow up (v.)
happiness (n.)
high (adj.)
hot (adj.)

interesting (adj.)
large (adj.)
local (n.)
mixture (n.)
modern (adj.)
nation (n.)
night spot (n.)
noisy (adj.)
poor (adj.)
region (n.)
ride (n.)
roller coaster (n.)
rural (adj.)
safe (adj.)
scenery (n.)
single (adj.)
small (adj.)
spectacular (adj.)
sunny (adj.)
take part in (v.)
ties (n.)

traffic (n.)
warm (adj.)
winter (n.)

Expressions
far away from
In my opinion….
(Maybe) you're
right.

Word for Word

Unit 10: On the job

above (prep.)
accountant (n.)
attorney (n.)
bay (n.)
below (prep.)
blind (adj.)
blindfold (n.)
boring (adj.)
bridge (n.)
careful (adj.)
cell phone (n.)
choose (v.)
client (n.)
colleague (n.)
commute (n.)
company (n.)
computer technician
  (n.)
condition (n.)
cost (n.)

difficult (adj.)
driving instructor (n.)
e-mail (n., v.)
end (n.)
engineer (n.)
flexible (adj.)
fog (n.)
foggy (adj.)
full-time (adj.)
guide dog (n.)
heating (n.)
ice cream vendor (n.)
impossible (adj.)
lawyer (n.)
mechanic (n.)
mobile (adj.)
mobile phone (n.)
mountain (n.)
musician (n.)
necessary (adj.)

ocean (n.)
paint (n., v.)
painter (n.)
part-time (adj.)
predict (v.)
professional (n.)
receptionist (n.)
rental car (n.)
safety equipment (n.)
save (v.)
schedule (n.)
security (n.)
space (n.)
start (v.)
street performer (n.)
stressful (adj.)
suit (n.)
taxi driver (n.)
telecommuter (n.)
telecommuting (n.)

trainer (n.)
training (n.)
T-shirt (n.)
understand (v.)
unnecessary (adj.)
virtual (adj.)
well-paid (adj.)
window dresser (n.)
windy (adj.)
worldwide (adj.)
zoo keeper (n.)

Expressions
Can I…?
Do you mind if I…?
Go ahead.
in contact
Is it OK to…?
Yes, of course.

Unit 11: Personal style

appearance (n.)
beard (n.)
black (adj.)
blonde (adj.)
blouse (n.)
blue (adj.)
briefcase (n.)
brown (adj.)
casual (adj.)
coat (n.)
conservative (adj.)
curly (adj.)
dark (adj.)
delicate (adj.)
develop (v.)
disappointment (n.)
dress (n.)
eyes (n.)
face (n.)
fashionable (adj.)
figure (n.)

formal (adj.)
friendship (n.)
gray (adj.)
hair (n.)
hat (n.)
heart (n.)
jacket (n.)
jeans (n.)
jewelry (n.)
kind (n., adj.)
leather (n.)
library (n.)
light (adj.)
long (adj.)
middle-aged (adj.)
mind (n.)
mustache (n.)
note (n.)
notice (v.)
overweight (adj.)
pale (adj.)

pants (n.)
personality (n.)
red (adj.)
refuse (v.)
rose (n.)
round (adj.)
scarf (n.)
shirt (n.)
shoes (n.)
short (adj.)
skin (n.)
skirt (n.)
slim (adj.)
smile (v.)
sneakers (n.)
straight (adj.)
style (n.)
tall (adj.)
test (n., v.)
thin (adj.)
tie (n.)

T-shirt (n.)
uncomfortable (adj.)
white (adj.)

Unit 12: Plans and ambitions

bank clerk (n.)
become (v.)
career (n.)
college (n.)
computer
  programming (n.)
continuing education
  (n.)
correction (n.)
definitely (adv.)
degree (n.)
doctor (n.)
education (n.)
enrolled (adj.)
eventually (adv.)
exam (n.)
experience (n.)
field (n.)
flight attendant (n.)
give up (a job) (v.)

get (a job) (v.)
improve (v.)
information systems
  (n.)
international business
  (n.)
investment banker (n.)
keep up with (v.)
legal assistant (n.)
make money (v.)
paragraph (n.)
pass (v.)
plan (n., v.)
priority (n.)
probably (adv.)
skill (n.)
start a family (v.)
take (v.)
time off (v.)
think (v.)

train (v.)
university (n.)
professor (n.)

Expressions
follow his dreams

Unit 13: Social life

admit (v.)
age (n.)
alternative (adj.)
announce (v.)
anybody (pron.)
anything (pron.)
anywhere (adv.)
ask someone out (v.)
attend (v.)
attitude (n.)
background (n.)
best friend (n.)
break up (v.)
businessman (n.)
button (n.)
call (v.)
contribution (n.)
date (n.)
discuss (v.)
event (n.)
everyone (pron.)

everything (pron.)
everywhere (adv.)
favor (n.)
friendly (adj.)
get along (v.)
get together (v.)
go out with (v.)
help (v.)
honest (adj.)
interest (n.)
introduce (v.)
invite (v.)
lazy (adj.)
lend (v.)
monthly (adj.)
night club (n.)
no one (n.)
nothing (n.)
nowhere (adv.)
open-minded (adj.)
opposites (n.)

optimistic (adj.)
outgoing (adj.)
outspoken (adj.)
positive (adj.)
promise (v.)
relationship (n.)
reliable (adj.)
romantic (adj.)
shout (v.)
shy (adj.)
similar (adj.)
singles (n.)
someone (pron.)
something (pron.)
somewhere (adv.)
spend time (v.)
stubborn (adj.)
upset (v)

Expressions
Could you…?

easy to talk to
fun to be with
in trouble
sense of humor
Would you mind…?

Unit 14: Future trends

advance (n.)
alarm (n.)
attached (adj.)
believe (v.)
belt (n.)
body (n.)
browse (v.)
cash (n.)
CD player (n.)
collar (n.)
communicate (v.)
connect (v.)
credit card (n.)
data (n.)
download (v.)
fabric (n.)
future (n.)
give (v.)
handheld (adj.)
heart rate (n.)

hospital (n.)
illness (n.)
information (n.)
intelligent (adj.)
keyboard (n.)
measure (v.)
message (n.)
mini-computer (n.)
mouse (n.)
online (adj., adv.)
outfit (n.)
pager (n.)
planet (n.)
printer (n.)
receive (v.)
scanner (n.)
screen (n.)
send (v.)
sensor (n.)
show (v.)

software (n.)
speak (v.)
technology (n.)
tell (v.)
temperature (n.)
thief (n.)
traffic (n.)
type (v.)
VCR (n.)
video (n.)
voice mail (n.)
web site (n.)
workout (n.)
World Wide Web
    (n.)

Unit 15: Lifetime achievements

afraid (*adj.*)
alive (*adj.*)
amazed (*adj.*)
anniversary (*n.*)
appear (*v.*)
article (*n.*)
celebration (*n.*)
experience (*n.*)
fantasy (*n.*)
farm (*n.*)
fear (*n.*)
fly (*v.*)
former (*adj.*)
goal (*n.*)
graduation (*n.*)
learn to (*v.*)
lifelong (*adj.*)
lifetime (*n.*)
lottery (*n.*)
love (*v.*)

lover (*n.*)
marathon (*n.*)
medal (*n.*)
natural (*adj.*)
overseas (*adv.*)
philosopher (*n.*)
remember (*v.*)
risk (*n.*)
rock climbing (*n.*)
run (*v.*)
scuba diving (*n.*)
specific (*adj.*)
start a business (*v.*)
surfing (*n.*)
take up (*v.*)
trapeze (*n.*)
well (*adv.*)
win (*v.*)
young (*adj.*)

Expressions
around the world
Congratulations!
good luck
Happy birthday!
Happy anniversary!
raise a family

Word for Word

Unit 16: Hobbies and habits

arm (*n.*)
artist (*n.*)
back (*n.*)
badminton (*n.*)
ball (*n.*)
baseball (*n.*)
basketball (*n.*)
bat (*n.*)
battery (*n.*)
bend (*v.*)
biking (*n.*)
both (*adj.*)
breathe (*v.*)
camera (*n.*)
cap (*n.*)
chess (*n.*)
decorate (*v.*)
diving (*n.*)
draw (*v.*)
factory (*n.*)

focus (*v.*)
finger (*n.*)
foot / feet (*n.*)
free time (*n.*)
hand (*n.*)
head (*n.*)
heel (*n.*)
horse (*n.*)
instrument (*n.*)
kick (*v.*)
knee (*n.*)
leg (*n.*)
magazine (*n.*)
marble (*n.*)
mouth (*n.*)
neck (*n.*)
nose (*n.*)
parade (*n.*)
pastime (*n.*)
pedal (*n., v.*)

press (*v.*)
push off (*v.*)
racket (*n.*)
running (*n.*)
shoulder (*n.*)
side (*n.*)
skateboarding (*n.*)
skiing (*n.*)
soccer (*n.*)
sport (*n.*)
stomach (*n.*)
swimming (*n.*)
take off (*v.*)
tennis (*n.*)
vehicle (*n.*)
volleyball (*n.*)
wheel (*n.*)
yoga (*n.*)

Expressions
current affairs

Word for Word

Grammar Reference

This section summarizes the main grammar points presented in this book.

Simple present: be — Unit 1

Affirmative

Subject	be		Subject	be	
I	am	fine.	We	are	colleagues.
You	are	from Peru.	You	are	students.
He					
She	is	from Seattle.	They	are	neighbors.
It					

Negative

Subject	be + not		Subject	be + not	
I	am not	a student.	We	are not	neighbors.
You	are not	American.	You	are not	colleagues.
He					
She	is not	late.	They	are not	students.
It					

Contractions: be (present)

Affirmative

I'm	he's
you're	she's
we're	it's
they're	

Negative

I'm not
he /she isn't *or* he's /she's not
it isn't *or* it's not
you aren't *or* you're not
we aren't *or* we're not
they aren't *or* they're not

Simple past: be — Unit 16

Affirmative

Subject	be		Subject	be	
I	was	late.	We	were	happy.
You	were	at work.	You	were	at home.
He					
She	was	busy	They	were	famous.
It					

Negative

Subject	be + not		Subject	be + not	
I	was not	late	We	were not	at home.
You	were not	at home.	You	were not	busy.
He					
She	was not	happy.	They	were not	late
It					

Contractions: be (past)

Affirmative

There are no contractions for the affirmative forms of *be* in the past.

Negative

I wasn't
you weren't
we weren't
they weren't
he /she / it wasn't

There is / are — Unit 4

Singular		Plural	
There is	a book on the desk.	There are	three books on the desk.
There isn't	a book on the desk.	There aren't	any books on the desk.
Questions		**Answers**	
Is there	a book on the desk?	Yes, there is. / No, there isn't.	
Are there	books on the desk?	Yes, there are. / No, there aren't.	

Don't confuse *there are, they are,* and *their. **There are** ten students in the class. **They're** learning English. **Their** books are new.*

Present continuous — Unit 5

Singular			Plural		
Subject	**be**	**Verb + -ing**	**Subject**	**be**	**Verb + -ing**
I	am	working.	We	are	working.
You	are	working.	You	are	working.
He					
She	is	working.	They	are	working.
It					

Negative: *be + not* + verb + *-ing*   *You **are not** (aren't) working.*

Simple present — Unit 2

Singular		Plural	
Subject	**Verb**	**Subject**	**Verb**
I	work.	We	work.
You	work.	You	work.
He			
She	works.	They	work.
It			

Negative: *do / does + not (don't, doesn't)* + verb
*You **don't work** on Fridays.*
*She **doesn't work** at home.*

Simple past — Units 6, 8

Singular		Plural	
Subject	**Verb**	**Subject**	**Verb**
I	worked.	We	worked.
You	worked.	You	worked.
He			
She	worked.	They	worked.
It			

Negative: *did not (didn't)* + verb
*We **didn't work** yesterday.*
*He **didn't work** last week.*

After the auxiliaries *do, does, did*, use the base form of the verb.

Present perfect — Unit 15

Singular				Plural			
Subject	**have / has**	**Past participle**		**Subject**	**have / has**	**Past participle**	
I	have	eaten	dinner.	We	have	had	lunch.
You	have	read	this book.	You	have	bought	new shoes.
He							
She	has	gone	away.	They	have	started	a business.
It							

Negative: *have / has + not (haven't / hasn't)* + past participle
*He **hasn't gone** away.*   *They **haven't started** a new business.*

Modal auxiliary verbs — Units 8, 14

Subject	Auxiliary verb	Verb	
Kelly	can	speak	Japanese.
He	could	swim	across the lake.
We	might	go out	tonight.
Runners	should	drink	a lot of water.
I	will	break	a record.
Greg	would rather	play	soccer.

Verb + *to* + verb — Units 10, 12

Subject	Verb + to + verb	
They	(would) like to travel	to Antarctica.
My father	wants to read	the newspaper.
They	(would) prefer to play	computer games.
Keith	has to cook	dinner.
Jack and Bob	plan to graduate	in June.

Be going to — Unit 12

I	am going to get	a new job.
He	is going to play	computer games.
They	are going to eat	breakfast.

Verbs with two objects — Unit 14

	Indirect object	Direct object
My brother gave	me	this computer.
Carol bought	us	some hamburgers.

	Direct object	Indirect object
He gave	it	to me.
She bought	them	for us.

Don't use an indirect object pronoun followed by a direct object pronoun. ~~He gave me it~~.

Auxiliaries + *too / either* — Unit 16

Affirmative response		Negative response	
Statement	Auxiliary + too	Statement	Auxiliary + either
I like basketball.	I do too.	I don't like baseball.	I don't either.
She ate dinner.	He did too.	They didn't eat lunch.	We didn't either.
We are tired.	I am too.	I'm not hungry.	We aren't either.
They were working.	We were too.	My friends weren't late.	I wasn't either.

Question	
Do you like to exercise?	I don't, but my boyfriend does.
Does David go to the gym?	He did, but now he doesn't.

Expressing purpose and reasons: *to* and *because* — Unit 12

	to	Verb	
I go to the gym	to	exercise.	

	because	Subject	Verb	
Chris is drinking water	because	he	is	thirsty.

Questions: *be*			Units 1, 8
Wh- questions			
Question word	*Verb*		
What	is	your name?	
Where	was	the concert?	

Yes / No *questions*			**Yes / No** *answers*		
Verb	*Subject*		*Yes / No*	*Subject*	*Verb*
Are	you	single?	Yes,	I	am.
Was	he	on time?	No,	he	wasn't.

You can use a noun or an adjective after *be*.

Questions: **Present continuous and *be going to***			Units 5, 10	
Wh- questions				
Question word	*be*	*Subject*		
Why	are	you	calling	her?
When	is	she	going to wash	the dishes?

Yes / No *questions*			**Yes / No** *answers*		
be	*Subject*		*Yes / no*	*Subject*	*Verb*
Is	your sister	eating?	No,	she	isn't.
Are	you	going to exercise?	Yes,	I	am.

Don't forget to finish *be going to* sentences with the base form of a verb.

***Wh*- questions**				Units 2, 6, 8, 10, 13
Question word	*Auxiliary verb*	*Subject*	*Verb*	
Where	do	you	work?	
When	did	he	arrive?	
How much	can	they	buy?	
Where	could	they	go?	
Why	should	we	leave?	
Where	would	you	rather live?	

Subject questions			***Object questions***			
Subject	*Verb*	*Object*	*Object*	*Auxiliary verb*	*Subject*	*Verb*
Who	believes	him?	Who	does	he	believe?
Who	met	Laura?	Who	did	Laura	meet?

Most English speakers use *who* (not *whom*) for object questions.

Yes / No questions — Units 2, 6, 8, 10, 15

Questions				Answers		
Auxiliary verb	Subject	Verb		Yes / no	Subject	Verb
Does	she	have	a cell phone?	Yes,	she	does.
Did	he	work	late?	No,	he	didn't.
Have	you	done	your work?	Yes,	we	have.
Can	they	eat	roast beef?	No,	they	can't.
Could	he	swim?		Yes,	he	could.
Should	we	dress	warmly?	Yes,	you	should.
Will	you	do	me a favor?	No,	I	won't.
Would	you	rather stay?		Yes,	I	would.

Countable nouns / Uncountable nouns — Unit 7

Countable nouns	Uncountable nouns
How many books did you read last month?	**How much coffee** do you drink?
I read **one book**.	I drink a lot of **coffee**.
Sarah read **four books**.	My mother drinks **two cups of coffee** after dinner.*

*To "count" an uncountable noun, use an expression of quantity, for example, *two cups of*.
Some uncountable nouns are used in the plural to indicate more than one kind of the item.
They served three different cheeses at the party.

Modifiers — Unit 7

How much coffee did you make?	**How many** copies did you make?	**How big** is the office?
I made **too much** coffee.	I made **too many** copies.	It's **too big**!
I made **a lot** of coffee.	I made **a lot** of copies.	It's **very big**.
I made **enough** coffee.	I made **enough** copies.	It's **big enough**.
I made **some** coffee.	I made **some** copies.	It's **pretty big**.
I did**n't** make **much** coffee.	I did**n't** make **many** copies.	It's **not very big**.
I did**n't** make **enough** coffee.	I did**n't** make **enough** copies.	It's **not big enough**!
I did**n't** make **any** coffee!	I did**n't** make **any** copies!	

Pronouns and possessive forms — Units 1, 11, 14

Subject pronouns	Object pronouns	Possessive adjectives	Possessive pronouns	Possessive 's
I	me	my	mine	
you	you	your	yours	
he	him	his	his	John's
she	her	her	hers	Sally's
it	it	its	its	
we	us	our	ours	
you	you	your	yours	
they	them	their	theirs	Tim and Nan's

To show that a plural noun is possessive, add an apostrophe (') after the final -s. *The teachers' books are red.*
If the plural noun does not end in -s (*children, people*), add 's. *The children's chairs are small.*
If two people own one object, you can say, for example, *Tim and Nan's car.*

Demonstratives Unit 4

	As adjectives	As pronouns
Near	This picture is beautiful.	This is a beautiful picture.
	These cars are old.	These are old cars.
Far	That cat is black.	That is a black cat.
	Those buildings are tall.	Those are tall buildings.

Degree of adjectives Unit 9

	Regular	(1 syllable)	(2 or more syllables)	Irregular
Comparative	(+ -er or more)	Maria is tall. John is taller.	These are beautiful cats. Those cats are more beautiful.	good, bad better, worse
Superlative	(+ -est or most)	Paul is the tallest.	This cat is the most beautiful.	best, worst

For adjectives ending in *y*, change the *y* to *-ier* for the comparative and *-iest* for the superlative forms.

Expressions of frequency and time Unit 3

I **always** shower **in the morning**.
I am **usually** busy **during the week**.
I **often** eat eggs for breakfast.
I **sometimes** read the newspaper.
I **hardly ever** watch TV.
I am **never** late for work.
On weekends I sleep late.
Once a week on Saturdays, I go to yoga class.
I meet friends for dinner **twice a month**.
Three times a year, I visit my parents in Florida.

The position of the adverb of frequency depends on the type of sentence.
Sentence with *be*: She is *always* tired at night.
Sentence with a regular verb: I *hardly ever* watch TV.
In negative sentences, adverbs usually go between the auxiliary and the main verb:
I don't *usually* stay out late.

Adverbs of manner Unit 16

	Verb		Adverb
She	eats		quickly.
I	did	my homework	carefully.
They	cleaned	the house	well.
The artist	paints		beautifully.

Irregular Verbs

Base form	Simple past	Past participle	Base form	Simple past	Past participle
be	was	been	leave	left	left
beat	beat	beaten	make	made	made
become	became	become	meet	met	met
bend	bent	bent	put	put	put
break	broke	broken	read	read	read
buy	bought	bought	ride	rode	ridden
cast	cast	cast	ring	rang	rung
choose	chose	chosen	run	ran	ran
come	came	come	say	said	said
cut	cut	cut	see	saw	seen
do	did	done	sell	sold	sold
draw	drew	drawn	send	sent	sent
drink	drank	drunk	sing	sang	sung
drive	drove	driven	sit	sat	sat
eat	ate	eaten	sleep	slept	slept
fight	fought	fought	speak	spoke	spoken
find	found	found	spend	spent	spent
fly	flew	flown	stand	stood	stood
get	got	gotten	steal	stole	stolen
give	gave	given	swim	swam	swum
go	went	gone	take	took	taken
grow	grew	grown	teach	taught	taught
have	had	had	tell	told	told
hide	hid	hidden	think	thought	thought
hit	hit	hit	throw	threw	thrown
hold	held	held	understand	understood	understood
hurt	hurt	hurt	wear	wore	worn
keep	kept	kept	win	won	won
know	knew	known	write	wrote	written

Audioscripts

This section provides audioscripts where a reference and extra support for recorded activities may be helpful.

Unit 1

9b-c

A = Alan, B = Betty

A: Hi. I'm Alan Hansen.
B: I'm Betty Mendez.
A: Mendez…. Are you Joe's sister?
B: No, I'm his cousin. My father and his father are brothers.
A: Well, it's very nice to meet you! Welcome to Los Angeles!
B: Thank you. Are you umm…in Emily's family or umm…?
A: Oh, Joe and I are colleagues. We're in the same office.
B: Oh, I see. Well, it's very nice to meet you! Are you from California?
A: No. Actually, I'm from Denmark.
B: Really? Your English is very good!
A: Well, my wife is American. I speak English at home.
B: Oh, I see. Is that your wife over there?
A: No! My wife's not here. That's my daughter.
B: Your daughter? Really?
A: Yes.

Unit 2

6a-b

I = Interviewer, Ta = Tina, Tm = Tom, E = Eric
1   I: How do you get to work?
    Ta: I drive.
    I: How long does it take?
    Ta: In the mornings, about 90 minutes. In the evenings, about two hours.
    I: That's a lot! What time do you leave in the mornings?
    Ta: About five o'clock.
    I: Don't you get bored?
    Ta: Not really. I relax, listen to music…. I like driving, so it's not so bad.
2   I: How do you get to work?
    Tm: I take the subway.
    I: Every day?
    Tm: Yes. Every day.
    I: Do you like it?
    Tm: No, I hate it. The trains are always late. Sometimes it takes an hour to get home.

I: What do you do on the train?
Tm: Nothing. I sleep, if I get a seat.
3   I: How do you get to work?
    E: Well, I don't have a car, so I ride my bicycle.
    I: You ride a bike downtown? Don't you feel nervous?
    E: No! It's the only way to get around. No problems parking!
    I: What do you do when it rains?
    E: When it rains I take a bus—but it takes much longer.

11a

Aa = Alicia, At = Agent
Aa: Excuse me.
At: Yes, can I help you?
Aa: Is this the bus to Portland?
At: Yes, it is.
Aa: When does it leave?
At: 10:30.
Aa: OK, thank you. Oh…how long does it take?
At: Four hours and ten minutes.
Aa: Thank you very much.

Unit 3

5b-c

This is WKYK, your favorite music station, with your guide to entertainment in the city this weekend. First of all, we have the Summer in the City Celebration. Good food and live music all day long. There's entertainment for the children, too. It's at Washington Park, Saturday and Sunday from 10 a.m. to 5 p.m. So come along and bring the family!
Also continuing at the Paramount Theater is the popular Broadway show, *Get Up and Go*. Performances are at 8 p.m. daily and 2 p.m. on Sunday. I recommend this one, folks—the singing and dancing are really wonderful. Go see it now, before it closes! That's at the Paramount Theater at 550 Stone Street. For tickets and information call 455-3899.
Finally, if you love the blues, on Saturday night Della Thompson performs live at the Blue Moon Club on Blake Street at nine o'clock. Tickets are on sale at Delta Records and Tickettrax. Fifteen dollars general admission, ten dollars for students. Check it out! And that's it for…

Unit 4

8a-b

E = Ellen, M = Man

E: Hello. I'm interested in the house for rent.

M: Ah, yes.

E: I have a question, umm…where is the house exactly?

M: It's in ***

E: I'm sorry. Could you repeat that, please? The line is bad.

M: Tortola. In the Virgin Islands.

E: Umm…. How do you spell that?

M: T-O-R-T-O-L-A. It's in the Virgin Islands.

E: Thank you. And umm…how many bedrooms are there?

M: *** bedrooms.

E: I'm sorry. Did you say two bedrooms or three?

M: Three. There are three bedrooms. But…

E: How many bathrooms are there?

M: Two bathrooms. But it's…

E: And is it near a town?

M: No. There aren't any large towns on the island. It's near the beach. But…

E: How far is it from the airport?

M: About five miles. But the house ***

E: I'm sorry, I don't understand.

M: It's not available. The house is not available.

E: Oh! I'm sorry.

M: That's OK.

Unit 5

1b-d

A = Airport announcer, W = Woman, M = Man

1 A: International Airlines Flight 345 to Hong Kong is now boarding. Would passengers please proceed to gate 53. Flight 345 to Hong Kong is now boarding at Gate 53.

W: Excuse me…

M: Yes?

W: What's happening with the flight to Boston? I'd like some information.

M: The Boston flight is canceled, ma'am.

W: Oh, no! Why?

M: It's snowing in Boston, and the airport is closed.

W: But how…what…?

M: Please take a seat, ma'am. We're putting people on flights to New York.

2 W: Excuse me! I'm looking for my suitcase, and I don't see it.

M: Where are you coming from?

W: Mexico City.

M: They're putting some baggage from Mexico City over there.

W: Oh yes. There it is. Thanks!

3 W: There's a man here…. He's from Germany, and he has a dog with him. He's traveling to Los Angeles. I'm looking at his papers. He doesn't have papers for the dog.

M: What? He doesn't have any papers at all?

W: No.

M: Oh, brother. Where is he right now?

W: He's standing right here.

M: OK. I'll be right there.

8b

M = Mike, S = Sue

M: Excuse me. I'm looking for the restrooms.

S: They're on the second floor. Go straight up the escalator and turn left.

M: Thank you.

Unit 6

1b-d

Part 1

Today we're talking about time management. Time management is about how you manage your time. A lot of people don't use their time very well.

Let's look at an example. I have a friend. Let's say his name is Robert. He's a manager at a bank. Robert has a problem with time. He has a lot of work to do, and he can never finish everything. He says he doesn't have time.

Now, if you look at Robert's time journal for last Thursday morning, March 17th, you'll see why he has a problem.

Part 2

Last Thursday Robert arrived at work at 8:30. He sat down and turned on the computer. He read and answered his e-mail messages for about 30 minutes. At 9:00 he checked the business news on the Internet. But he didn't just read the business news. He read the sports news too. He found some interesting information about his favorite basketball team.

After that he wanted some coffee. He left the office at 9:30 and went to a coffee shop a few blocks away. That took some time. On the way back, he met a colleague. He talked to her about a problem she had with her car. It was 10:15 before he got back to the office.

Then an employee asked Robert about a problem with his computer program. So Robert spent 45 minutes helping him.

At 11:00 Robert still had not done any of his own work! And we all have days like this!

10a

M = Molly, J = John

M: I'm sorry I'm late.

J: What happened?

M: I was in a meeting at work, and it didn't finish until six.

J: Don't worry about it.

Unit 7

2c

1 a slice of bread, a slice of cheese, a slice of pizza
2 a glass of mineral water, a glass of soda, a glass of milk, a glass of juice
3 a bowl of soup, a bowl of cereal, a bowl of fruit
4 a can of fruit, a can of soda, a can of soup

4b-c

H = Host, D = Doctor

H: Doctor, what do you think of the American diet?

D: Well, it's much better than it was. People are making some good changes. But we still eat a lot of fat and salty snacks. And all that's bad for your heart.

H: All the things I like. So all the good things are bad for you, right?

D: Yes, certainly a lot of good tasting things are bad for you. But some are good for you. Look at the Mediterranean diet, for example. It's a very healthy diet, but it's good food, too.

H: But how is that diet so different from typical American food?

D: Oh, Americans still cook with a lot of butter. The Mediterranean diet uses olive oil in cooking and more fruits and vegetables. Not as many desserts. Americans love sugar: desserts, cakes, ice cream…and so on.

H: What about the Asian diet?

D: A traditional Asian diet is even better. A lot of vegetables and fish. Of course, there's quite a lot of salt in some Asian dishes, but it is still a very healthy diet.

H: Mmm.

D: But you know, it's hard to speak of a traditional diet any more. People's habits are changing. Many people don't eat a "traditional diet." And American-style fast food is popular everywhere.

10a

W = Waiter, C = Customer

W: Are you ready to order?

C: Yes, please. I'll have the salmon.

W: Salmon, OK.

C: Does that come with vegetables?

W: It comes with potatoes and a small salad.

C: That sounds good.

W: Would you like something to drink?

C: Yes. Could I have some mineral water, please?

W: Yes, of course.

Unit 8

3c

And finally tonight, some international news. A French swimmer arrived back in France yesterday after swimming there—all the way from the United States. Benoît Lecomte, 31, swam across the Atlantic Ocean in 72 days. He swam six to eight hours a day and slept on a boat at night. Lecomte raised $175,000 for medical research.

8b-c

I love old things, so I often spend time in antique stores. Well, one day I went to one of my favorite stores because I wanted to buy a vase. I saw some vases in the window, so I went inside and started looking around. I spent quite a long time in there. After a while, I found a vase that I liked. Then I went to pay for my vase, but I couldn't see the sales person. So I called out, "Umm, excuse me!" but nobody came. I realized I was alone in the store.

Unit 9

2b-c

J = Joe, C = Christina, F = Fernanda

J: OK. Say "cheese."

C&F: "Cheese!"

C: Thanks for taking our picture.

J: Where are you from?

C&F: Santiago—in Chile.

J: Are you on vacation in Chicago?

C: Fernanda is. I live here. She's visiting me. Sorry. My name is Christina. This is my cousin, Fernanda.

J: Hi. I'm Joe.

C&F: Nice to meet you.

J: Do you like Chicago, Christina?

C: I love it here. It's a really exciting city to live in. There's so much to see and do.

J: Why did you come to the United States?

C: I got a job working for a bank here in Chicago.

J: Do you live in the city?

C: Yes. I live on First Street.

J: Oh, that's a nice neighborhood.

C: Yes, it is. It's very convenient. I can walk to work.

J: What about you, Fernanda? Would you like to live here?

F: No! I think she's crazy. No, no, she's not crazy, but I couldn't live in Chicago. It's too cold in the winter.

J: What's it like in Santiago?

F: Oh, I love Santiago. It's a beautiful city. It's smaller than Chicago, but has more people. There are plenty of things to do. It's my home! All of my family and friends are there.

3c

1 Tokyo is larger than Sydney.
2 Mexico City is higher than Amsterdam.
3 San Francisco is smaller than London.
4 Dallas is more modern than Rome.
5 São Paulo is bigger than Bangkok.
6 Moscow is colder than Miami.

Unit 10

9b-c

I = Interviewer, E = Emily

I: What do you have to do, Emily, if you want to be a guide dog trainer?
E: Well, there's a training program.
I: And how long does that take?
E: About three years. And at the beginning, you have to wear a blindfold for ten days.
I: Wow. All day?
E: Twenty-four hours a day, yes. That way, you begin to understand what it's like to be blind.
I: Yes, of course.
E: Then you start working with the dogs. You have to teach them about traffic, crowds, escalators, buses…so you take them out every day. You're on your feet all day…in all weather! Rain, snow….
I: It sounds like very hard work.
E: It is. It's hard, physically. You get a lot of exercise.
I: How long does it take to train a dog?
E: About six months.
I: And do you work with just the dogs?
E: At first we work with just the dogs. At the end of the program, we introduce the dogs to their new owners. Then we work with them together for the last month.
I: What do you like about the job?
E: When you see a dog working with a blind person for the first time, it's fantastic. That's when I know I love my job.

Unit 11

1b

1 He's wearing a red shirt and a white sweater. He's also wearing a hat.
2 She's wearing a blue sweater and black pants.
3 She's wearing a dress with flowers on it.
4 He's wearing brown pants. He's also wearing a sweater and a scarf.

2b-c

I = Interviewer, R = Richard

I: I'd like to ask you about the clothes you wear. You have a very classic style.
R: Well, yes, I have to wear dark suits.
I: That's very conservative.
R: You have to look conservative when you're an attorney. You can't wear anything that's too fashionable.
I: Why not?
R: People don't trust you. Also, you don't want people focusing on your clothes. You want them to listen to what you have to say.
I: Hmm. That's interesting.
R: I try to wear interesting ties.
I: How many ties do you have?
R: Oh, lots. I don't know. I guess I have about 50 I regularly wear.
I: So you always wear a suit and tie.
R: Most of the time, yes. Sometimes, if I'm just working in the office, I wear more casual clothes.
I: Really? Like what?
R: Well… khakis and a sports jacket.
I: What about weekends?
R: Oh, I'm really casual. I wear jeans and T-shirts. I wear a suit every day to work, so I don't wear a suit on the weekends.
I: Do you wear jewelry?
R: No. Just my wedding ring.
I: One more question. What's the oldest thing in your closet?
R: Oh…umm…let me think. Umm…probably my ski pants. They're ten years old. I hardly ever go skiing.

4

A = Alex, E = Eva

A: What do you think of this jacket?
E: It's very nice, but I don't think it's big enough.
A: Hmm. Yes.
E: Maybe you should look for a larger one.
A: That's a good idea…
 And which pants should I buy?
E: Why don't you buy those? They look good.
A: They're not too long?
E: I don't think so.

Unit 12

7a-b

I1 = Interviewer #1, I2 = Interviewer #2,
I3 = Interviewer #3, A = Actor

I1: Mr. Williams, can I ask you a few questions?
A: OK.
I1: Now that you are married, are you going to take some time off?

A: Oh yes, definitely.

I2: Do you plan to live in Hollywood?

A: Probably, yes. My work is here.

I3: Do you and your wife want to start a family?

A: Maybe. I don't know. Now, if you'll excuse me…

10b-c

I = Interviewer, B = Barry

I: Barry, why did you give up your job?

B: I was completely burned out. I couldn't do it any more.

I: But you're only 25.

B: I know, but I started work when I was 20, and I worked 100 hours a week. That's more than ten years of experience in five years.

I: How many hours did you say?

B: 100 hours a week. Sometimes I worked two or three days without sleeping. I was married to my job. I never saw my friends or my family. You can't do that forever. At some point you say, that's enough.

I: Hmm.

B: At the beginning, I didn't care. I just wanted to make a lot of money. And I did. Now my priorities are different.

I: What are you going to do now?

B: Well, I'm going to spend some time with my family first, and then in the spring I plan to go on a biking trip around Europe with a friend.

I: And after that?

B: I'm going to go to back to school to study drama. I want to be an actor.

I: Really? That's interesting.

B: It's just something I always wanted to do. And now I'm going to do it!

Unit 13

5b

L = Laura, C = Carol

L: Well? How was the party, Carol?

C: Great! I met a really nice guy.

L: Really? Who did you meet?

C: His name is Patrick. He works with computers, I think.

L: Oh, he's a friend of Joe's.

C: Yes. Joe introduced us. He works with him, I think.

L: Yes. They work together. Who invited him to the party?

C: Who invited who? Joe?

L: No, Patrick. Who invited Patrick?

C: I think Amanda did.

L: Oh, yes. She went out with him for a while.

C: Really? What happened?

L: They broke up. But they're still friends. Anyway, did you like him?

C: Yes! We got along really well. He asked me out!

L: Well!

C: Listen, let's get together for lunch tomorrow and I'll tell you all about it.

L: Sure.

7c

1 An outgoing person is friendly with many people.

2 An outspoken person says what he or she thinks.

3 An optimistic person has a positive attitude towards life.

4 A person with a sense of humor often makes people laugh.

5 A kind person helps other people.

6 An honest person tells the truth.

7 A lazy person doesn't like to work hard.

8 An open-minded person is open to new ideas.

9 A stubborn person doesn't like to change his or her plans.

10 A reliable person does what he or she promises.

Unit 14

4a-b

Mn = Man, Ma = Melissa

Mn: Hello?

Ma: Hi. This is Melissa.

Mn: Oh, hi, Melissa.

Ma: Can I speak to Leo, please?

Mn: I'm sorry. He's not here right now.

Ma: Oh. Umm…. Could you give him a message?

Mn: Of course.

Ma: Could you tell him I called? My number is 555-9266.

Mn: Just a minute. Let me write that down. 555-9266. OK. I'll tell him.

Ma: Thanks!

6b-c

R = Rachel, N = Noah, T = Tony

R: I sit in front of a computer all day at work. But I don't even have one at home. I don't really want one! If I need to get online I use the one in the office. I go online to get information. For example, last week I was looking for information on plane tickets to San Diego. And I sometimes buy books or music online. But I think people will always prefer to shop in real stores. I know I do.

N: I spend all my free time on my computer at home, listening to music or playing games. I can get online as well and talk to people in all different countries. It's really cool…. I use it for school, too, if I have to write a paper or something. You can get any kind of information you want on the Web.

I think it's great, especially for students. I think in the future, schools might just have computer centers instead of libraries. We won't need books.

T: I use my computer for other reasons. At my company we use e-mail all the time to communicate with customers. I work at an international company, and we have a system that connects the different offices—so we can all get the same information and get it fast. It's fantastic, really. But of course, everyone will need computer skills in the future. Even now, you can't get a job without computer skills.

Unit 16
7b-c

1 OK, now listen carefully. Kick gently with both legs. Gently! Sit forward. That's right. Relax…that's it! Keep your legs under you. Keep your heels down. Relax your arms, just go with the horse. You have to be calm so you don't scare the horse. That's it! Giddyup!

2 Sit on the floor and cross your legs. Breathe deeply. Now take your left foot and put it on top of your right leg. That's right. Now do the same thing with your right foot. Put it on top of your left leg. Good. Keep your back straight and your shoulders down. That's right. Now rest your hands lightly on your knees. Don't forget to breathe.

Text Acknowledgments

The publishers are grateful to the individuals and institutions named below for permission to include their materials in this book.

p. 2: Cooper-Price profile used by permission of the Cooper-Price family.

p. 18: "The rhythm is going to get you" by Alice Thomson. *The Daily Telegraph,* December 19, 2000. © Telegraph Group Limited.

p. 19: "An Unusual Office" used by permission of Peter Nelson of TreeHouse Workshop.

p. 37: From A GEOGRAPHY OF TIME by ROBERT LEVINE. Copyright © 1997 by Robert Levine. Reprinted by permission of Basic Books, a member of Perseus Books, L.L.C.

p. 40: Dictionary entry from the *American Wordpower Dictionary,* Ruth Urbom, ed. © 1998, Oxford University Press. ISBN 0-19-431319-0.

p. 42: "Researcher finds a way to budge TV-watching kids from sofa" by Lauran Neergaard. *Associated Press,* April 18, 1999. © Associated Press. Reprinted with permission of The Associated Press.

p. 43: Statistics reprinted with permission from *Amazing Almanac,* by Jenny Tesar. © 2000, Blackbirch Press Inc.

p. 47: "You might think our police are going nuts." *The Bath Chronicle,* May 31, 2002. © Northcliffe Electronic Publishing Ltd.

p. 50: "SILHOUETTES" by Frank Slay Jr. and Robert Crewe Copyright © 1957 by Regent Music Corporation (BMI) All Rights Reserved. Used By Permission. International Copyright Secured.

p. 56: "Science Tracks the Good Life" by Keay Davidson. *The San Francisco Chronicle,* December 24, 2000. © *The San Francisco Chronicle.* Reprinted with Permission.

p. 59: "Above it All" 2/95. © 1995 Time Inc. Reprinted by permission.

p. 61: "Anyway, anyhow, anywhere" by Jim Pollard. *The Guardian,* September 3, 2000. © Jim Pollard.

p. 64: Guide Dog Trainer information used by permission of Joanne Ritter of Guide Dogs for the Blind, Inc.

p. 70: "Appointment with Love" by S. I. Kishor. Reprinted with permission from the May 1951 Reader's Digest. Previously published in *This is America,* by Max J. Herzberg. Pocket Books, 1950. By permission of John Herzberg.

p. 79: "Looking for love? How about the local supermarket?" by Donna Abu-Nasr. *Associated Press,* September 8, 1997. © Associated Press. Reprinted with permission of The Associated Press.

p. 91: Sam Keen information used by permission of Sam Keen.

p. 95: IN MY LIFE Copyright © 1965 (renewed) Sony/ATV Songs LLC. All rights administered by Sony/ATV Music Publishing, 8 Music Square West, Nashville, TN 37203. All rights reserved. Used by permission.

p. 102: The Cat's Meow used by permission of Nicole Strine Goldman. The Garden Car used by permission of Keith Moss. Ron Dolce's Marble Madness used by permission of Harrod Blank of Art Car Agency.

OXFORD
UNIVERSITY PRESS

198 Madison Avenue
New York, NY 10016 USA

Great Clarendon Street
Oxford OX2 6DP England

Oxford University Press is a department of the University of Oxford.
It furthers the University's objective of excellence in research, scholarship,
and education by publishing worldwide in

Oxford New York

Auckland Cape Town Dar es Salaam Hong Kong Karachi
Kuala Lumpur Madrid Melbourne Mexico City Nairobi
New Delhi Shanghai Taipei Toronto

With offices in

Argentina Austria Brazil Chile Czech Republic France Greece
Guatemala Hungary Italy Japan Poland Portugal Singapore
South Korea Switzerland Thailand Turkey Ukraine Vietnam

OXFORD and OXFORD ENGLISH are registered trademarks of
Oxford University Press

Library of Congress Cataloging-in-Publication Data

Blackwell, Angela.
  English knowhow. Student book 1 / Angela Blackwell, Therese Naber ; with
Gregory J. Manin.
    p. cm.
  ISBN-13: 978 0 19 453673 8 (pbk.)

  1. English language—Textbooks for foreign speakers. I. Title: English knowhow
student book 1. II. Naber, Therese. III. Manin, Gregory J. IV. Title.

PE1128.B583 2003
428'.4—dc21

                       2003040551

Editorial Manager: Judith Cunningham
Design Project Manager: Maj-Britt Hagsted
Senior Designer: Claudia Carlson
Art Editor: Judi DeSouter
Production Manager: Shanta Persaud
Production Controller: Zai Jawat Ali

ISBN-13: 978 0 19 453864 0 (Student Book with CD)

ISBN-13: 978 0 19 453673 8 (Student Book without CD)

Printing (last digit): 10 9 8 7

Printed in Hong Kong.

ACKNOWLEDGEMENTS

Cover photographs: International Stock/ImageState (airport); Larry Lawfer/Index
Stock (woman on phone); PictureArts Corporation (trophy); VCG-Taxi/Getty
Images (straphanger)

Illustrations: Silke Bachmann pp. 23 (telephone scene), 51 (man), 69 (woman, man,
wig stands); Barbara Bastian pp. 15 (advertisements), 32 (article, chart), 37
(article), 44 (menus), 79 (article), 85 (chart), 90 (article), 96 (cards), 102 (article),
109 (time capsule); Ken Batelman p. 21 (tables, file cabinet), 60 (jobs), 99 (sports
icons); Annie Bissett pp. 7 (article), 17 (fancy letter), 23 (web sites), 24 (form), 39
(article), 58 (article), 59 (article), 71 (article), 83 (article); Dan Brown pp. 13 (people
at fountain), 29 (people at mall), 48 (beach scene, couple), 85 (two women), 86
(telephone scene), 97 (couple); Ken Dewar p. 40 (food); Patrick Faricy pp. 38
(couple), 55 (café, woman), 67 (shopping scenes), 81 (men), 82 (women), 101
(men); Erasmo Hernandez pp. 15 (entertainment scenes), 40 (bread, water, bowl,
can), 111 (island); Michael Hortens pp. 4 (computer screen), 21 (article), 57
(paragraph), 112 (game board), 116 (course list); Lene Idermark pp. 6 (party), 29
(restaurant); Susumu Kawabe pp. 10 (questionnaire), 33 (time journal), 46 (article),
61 (article), 73 (article), 76 (headline); Uldis Klavins pp. 20 (room), 31 (mall), 106
(floor plan), 108 (floor plan), 109 (floor plan); Gary McLaughlin pp. 64 (jobs), 70
(whole page), 77 (couple), 78 (couple), 114 (classroom); Karen Minot pp. 12
(notebook), 35 (journalist profile), 42 (e-mail), 45 (headlines), 56 (article), 62
(computer screen), 69 (descriptions), 72 (course listing), 75 (letter); Stephanie
O'Shaughnessy pp. 66 (store window), 74 (man with check), 92 (bank), 114
(problems); Alan Rabinowitz p. 87 (advertisement), 90 (woman); Rob Schuster
pp. 11 (article), 18 (article), 19 (article), 31 (mall entrance), 42 (article), 43
(clipping), 91 (interview); Don Stewart pp. 3 (people), 17 (telephone scene), 22
(couple), 27 (airport scenes), 28 (couple), 36 (two women), 49 (antique store
series), 63 (office), 68 (café), 74 (wedding), 93 (astronaut), 96 (anniversary, hospital,
exam); Anna Veltfort pp. 9 (subway car), 12 (airport, bus, car), 28 (airport
pictures), 68 (objects, parking lot), 81 (CD covers); John Ward pp. 41 (interview),
53 (two women and man), 103 (hockey family), 105 (outdoor scene)

Commissioned photographs: Angela Blackwell p. 2 (Cooper-Price family); Lyndall
Culbertson/Oxford University Press p. 1 (alarm clock); Stephen Ogilvy p. 1 (office
series); Jodi Waxman/Oxford University Press p. 21 (messy office, neat office).

*The publishers would like to thank the following for their permission to reproduce
photographs*: Action Plus p. 93 (marathon); George Ancona/International Stock p. 7
(subway); Associated Press p. 79 (supermarket); Scott Barrow/International Stock
p. 93 (raising children); Paul Barton/Corbis p. 65 (couple); Harrod Blank/Artcars
p. 102 (Ron Dolce's Marble Madness car); Mark Bolster/International Stock p. 66
(man); Pedro Coll/AGE Fotostock p. 113 (teenagers); Corbis pp. 7 (header), 13
(header, jazz band), 23 (Scotland), 25 (woman), 27 (header), 42 (girl), 45 (ice), 53
(header), 58 (Steel Dragon), 59 (header, man), 71 (header, Brazilian woman), 79
(header), 89 (people in line), 91 (header), 93 (guitar store), 97 (header); Comstock
Image$ p. 71 (Chinese boy); Peter DaSilva p. 91 (Sam Keen on trapeze); James
Davis/International Stock p. 116 (older man); Maria De Kord/International Stock
p. 85 (laptop); Paul DeMaio p. 11 (bike, bicyclist); Tony Demin/International Stock
p. 110 (rock climbing); Diamond/Ehlers/International Stock p. 61 (man); Eyewire
pp. 13 (dance club), 33 (header), 39 (header); Getty Images pp. 1 (header), 5
(brothers/sisters, three men, parents), 7 (man on phone, people on bus, ferry boat,
motorcycle), 8 (man), 9 (woman, man, bicyclist), 12 (family), 18 (woman), 19
(header), 23 (house interior), 33 (presentation), 36 (men), 37 (train), 45 (header), 65
(header, five people), 71 (man), 73 (woman), 76 (man), 85 (header, orange pager),
89 (watching TV), 90 (fire alarm, belt, fabric), 97 (tennis racket, soccer ball,
saxophone), 99 (badminton), 115 (camping), 116 (Hispanic woman); Michael
Girard/International Stock p. 53 (Chicago); Rick Gomez/AGE Fotostock p. 71 (Costa
Rican man); Hollenbeck Photography/International Stock p. 13 (couple at movies);
Hulton Archive p. 36 (fishing); The Image Bank pp. 5 (colleagues), (two men);
ImageState p. 35 (woman); Index Stock pp. 4 (man), 5 (boyfriend/girlfriend), 39
(supermarket), 99 (volleyball), 100 (horseback riding), 101 (swimming); K.H. Photo/
International Stock p. 85 (cell phone); Peter Langone/International Stock pp. 8
(woman), 71 (Swiss woman); Patti McConville/International Stock p. 24 (inside);
Peter McFarren/AP p. 58 (Bolivian hotel); John Michael /International Stock p. 85
(VCR); Yoshia Otsuka/Photonica p. 24 (outside); Photonica pp. 4 (woman), 7 (cable
car), 83 (boy, woman), 89 (traffic, woman on phone), 90 (shirt), 95 (couple), 97
(chess pieces), 99 (skateboarding, diving); Stone p. 30 (office, café, hat store);
Pacific Yurts Inc., 77456 Hwy 99 South, Cottage Grove, Oregon 97424,
www.yurts.com p. 26 (yurt); Michael Paras/International Stock pp. 83 (Dutch
woman), 116 (Asian woman); Lindy Powers/International Stock p. 13 (group
outside); Patrick Ramsey/International Stock pp. 13 (woman on sofa), 100 (yoga);
Reuters p. 46 (swimmer); George Shelley/Corbis p. 65 (four people); Christine
Shipp p. 91 (headshot of Sam Keen); Bill Stanton/International Stock p. 56
(family); Taxi pp. 18 (jogger), 44 (restaurant); Jay Thomas/International Stock p. 13
(exercising); Paul Thompson/International Stock p. 56 (Denmark); Ken Weingart/
International Stock p. 116 (young man); Dusty Willison/International Stock p. 101
(learning to bike); Brent Winebrenner/International Stock p. 53 (Chile)

Special thanks to: Pete Nelson p. 19 (tree house interior and exterior); West
Edmonton Mall p. 32 (ice rink, water); Betty T. Musso p. 36 (carriage); The Tourist
Office of Spain in New York p. 58 (La Tomatina); Guide Dogs for the Blind, Inc.
p. 64 (guide dogs); Keith Moss p. 102 (Garden Car)

*The authors and publishers extend thanks to the following English Language Teaching
professionals and institutions for their invaluable support and feedback during the
development of this series*: Gill Adams (Brazil); Virgílio Almeida and staff (Brazil);
Barbara Bangle (Mexico); Vera Berk (Brazil); James Boyd (Japan); Bonnie Brown de
Masis (Costa Rica); Janaína Cardoso and staff (Brazil); Hector Castillo (Mexico); Dr.
Robin Chapman (Japan); Nora Díaz (Mexico); Maria da Graça Duarte and staff
(Brazil); Stephen Edmunds (Mexico); Israel Escalante (Mexico); Raquel Farias and
staff (Brazil); Verónica Galván (Mexico); Saul Santos García (Mexico); Carmen
Gehrke and staff (Brazil); Arlete Würschig Gonçalves and staff (Brazil); Kimberley
Humphries (Mexico); Michelle Johnstone (Canada); Jean-Pierre Louvrier (Brazil);
Shan-jen Amy Lu (Taiwan); Mary Meyer (Paraguay); Dulce Montes de Oca (Mexico);
Harold Murillo (Colombia); Connie Reyes (Mexico); Carmen Oliveira and staff
(Brazil); Eliane Cunha Peixoto and staff (Brazil); Verónica Olguín (Mexico); Claudia
Otake (Mexico); Nicola Sarjeant (Korea); Débora Schisler and staff (Brazil); Lilian
Munhoz Soares and staff (Brazil); Sharon Springer (Costa Rica); Silvia Thalacker
and staff (Brazil); Kris Vicca (Taiwan); Daniel Zarate (Mexico); Ignacio Yepes (Mexico).
Centro Cultural Brasil-Estados Unidos, Santos; Centro de Línguas Estrangeiras
Mackenzie, São Paulo; ENEP Acatlán, Edo. de México; English Forever, Salvador;
Escola Técnica Estadual Fernando Prestes, Sorocaba; GreenSystem, Belo
Horizonte; IBEU, Rio; Instituto Cultural Brasil Norte-Americano, Porto Alegre;
MAI, Belo Horizonte; Plus!, Brasília; Quatrum, Porto Alegre; SENAC Rio; Seven,
São Paulo; Talkative, São Paulo; Universidade Autónoma de México; Universidad
Autónoma del Estado de México; Universidade Católica de Brasília; Universidad La
Salle, León, Guanajuato; Universidad Latino Americano, Mexico City; Universidad
Nacional Autónoma de México; Universidad Autónoma de Guadalajara.